More
Primary Literacy Centers

More
Primary Literacy Centers
Making Reading and Writing STICK!

Susan Nations & Mellissa Alonso

More Primary Literacy Centers
Making Reading and Writing STICK!

Cover and layout design: Mickey Cuthbertson
Photographers: Susan Nations and Mellissa Alonso
Editor: Emily Gorovsky

Contact both authors for inservice or consulting at www.literacycoaching.com or through the publisher.

Library of Congress Cataloging-in-Publication Data

Nations, Susan.
  More primary literacy centers : making reading and writing stick! / Susan
Nations & Mellissa Alonso.
      p. cm.
  Includes bibliographical references and index.
  ISBN-13: 978-0-929895-76-5 (pbk.)
  ISBN-10: 0-929895-76-2 (pbk.)
1. Language arts (Primary)--United States. 2. Classroom learning
centers--United States. I. Alonso, Mellissa, 1969- II. Title.
LB1529.U5N378 2006
372.6--dc22

                        2006023633

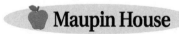

Maupin House publishes professional resources for K-12 educators. Contact us for tailored, in-school training or to schedule an author for a workshop or conference.
Visit www.maupinhouse.com for free lesson plan downloads.

Maupin House Publishing, Inc.
800-524-0634
352-378-5588
www.maupinhouse.com
10 9 8 7 6 5 4 3 2

Dedication

Dedicated to all those who help children discover their literate lives.

In memory of Bob Scholl for making real the world of informational text for young children.

Acknowledgments

It's hard to believe that this book project has taken over four years! Within these pages you will find the collaboration of countless teachers, staff developers, and children. We find that bringing a work like this to its completion is an arduous process. It requires getting in touch with our own pedagogy while being keenly aware of current trends in education. Classroom direction has changed dramatically over the past four years. There are more mandates, initiatives, and standards than ever. Teachers and students are being stretched into a new era of education.

We are deeply grateful to our publisher Maupin House for allowing us to bring this book to life. We especially want to thank our editor, Emily Gorovsky, for her hard work and dedication in editing this book. Her attention to detail is a gift for which we are grateful.

The children and teachers in the photos helped bring the literacy centers to life in this book! To Julie Collins and Erica Ross for allowing us to invade your classrooms for photos! And especially to Miss Collins' first-grade students, Miss Ross's second-grade students, and Mrs. Nations' third-grade students, thank you for showing us your hard work in centers and smiling again and again!

From Mellissa

The more I study the process of reading, the more I realize how much I still have yet to learn. Brenda Parkes has been and continues to be my source of inspiration as a teacher, coach, mentor, and friend. Her gentle, probing questions echo in my mind as I work with students and teachers on a daily basis. I stand in awe of her constant pursuit of quality literacy instruction for all children.

I am forever grateful to the Hillsborough County Reading Coach Project for continuing to invite me to be an integral part of their literacy development. This is the first project that has sustained eight years in our district. I am so proud of the teachers who have left the comfort of their classroom to accept the challenge of becoming Reading Coaches. Remember our role is to help others become comfortable with discomfort!

As a first-time administrator, I am honored to learn and grow alongside the faculty and staff of Esther D. Burney Elementary. You have welcomed me with open arms and you attend my trainings after long, exhausting, fulfilling days of teaching. You have been so patient with a new administrator who still thinks she teaches all day. My office looks more like a classroom than the "AP's office!" The Burney Bus is on its way.

My three beautiful children now range from preschool to college. Thank you, Miranda, for reminding me of the importance of snuggling at night with a good book and blanket. Thank you, Brianna, for juggling seven periods in the middle-school day with the grace of the skilled softball player you have become. Thank you, Tony, for showing me how college life without technology is so "old school, Mom!"

I have saved the best for last. To my husband, my babysitter, my resident chef, my life's partner, Hector. Your patience with me, and dedication to our family, define commitment. Thank you for your unconditional love, support, and reminders to call Susan and get this book finished!

From Susan

I must start by thanking my Principal, Steve Dragon, for allowing me to live out my passion for reading instruction daily. His dedication and commitment to children and their education is to be admired. The Gocio Elementary School staff helps me learn and grow each and every day as we collaborate to create meaningful literacy environments for students. Thank you for being MY teachers and making our school such a unique and special place!

To all the Literacy Coaches in Sarasota County for your conversations and investigations into best-practice teaching for all. A special thank you to Suzanne Naiman and Roni Harty for their support of the Literacy Coaching initiative in our district. They continue to spread the word that meaningful literacy centers are important for students as they develop their literate lives. To all of the Sarasota County staff developers and curriculum specialists who continue to support practical and applicable literacy implementation in our schools.

My own children inspire me each and every day. Thank you, Daniel, Matt, Jordan, and Aaron for your constant belief in the work I do. I know it is not always easy having such a crazy schedule, but you handle it with great patience and understanding. I love you all!

And to my best friend and husband, Don, for your commitment to my personal and professional growth. Your encouragement and belief in me is what keeps me going sometimes. You help me remember what is most important and keep perspective. I don't know where I'd be without you!

Table of Contents

Part One

Literacy Centers: Meaningful Practice in Action

Introduction: Reflections on Teaching and Learning

Students will happily engage in work that is connected to their lives and in projects which they can see value. As much as possible, ensure that the work students do is literacy-centered—that is, that students are reading and writing worthwhile texts that provide opportunities to expand their skills, knowledge, and thinking.

Regie Routman, *Reading Essentials: The Specifics You Need to Teach Reading Well* (203-204)

Sorting through the Questions

How can I make this more meaningful? What do I do if I run out of ideas? Why are my centers getting boring? The kids are finishing too fast—what do I do? Why aren't my students interested in my centers anymore? I spend a lot of time planning, so why do they finish so quickly? How do I get my students to read and write more in their centers? Should I be worried about the product or the process?

These are a just some of the questions that we hear from teachers when we present literacy center workshops around the country. Certainly there is no one right answer to any of these questions. But we hope this book will provide some answers and suggestions as you implement or refine meaningful literacy activities in your own classroom. Literacy centers truly are practice in action.

What's the Purpose Here?

Our purpose, as teachers, is to help our students meet the academic challenges they will face as they develop their literate lives. It is with this goal in mind that the literacy program in our classrooms must be designed. Our literacy instruction must be student-centered, data-driven (both informal and formal), and, most importantly, balanced.

Eyes on Students

If we want to build a classroom community where excellent teaching and learning take place, then it is our job to know our students. We have to ask ourselves what each student brings to the classroom academically, socially, emotionally, and experientially. Often the best lessons are inside the hearts and minds of our students just waiting to be explored. Routman discusses this need to bond in great detail in her book *Reading Essentials* (Heinemann, 2003). She notes that "unless we reach into our students' hearts, we have no entry into their minds."

In her book, *A Room with a Differentiated View* (Heinemann, 2004), JoAnne Yatvin notes that developing a sense of community is the most important management tool. We can only do this when we know who our students are and what they bring to this unique learning community. Yatvin states, "Teachers have considerable power to influence their students' attitudes and behavior, and it's worthwhile for them to exert that power to turn a group of strangers into a caring and respectful community" (29). This must be the goal of every teacher.

Finding out where students are academically tends to be the easy part. There are many surveys, inventories, formal and informal assessments, and interviews designed for this purpose. It is up to each teacher to research and find out which of these tools will give the information he or she needs to know about what students' know and are ready to learn.

Understanding the social, emotional, and experiential background of students is much more difficult. It requires that we take the time to actually have conversations with individuals as well as small groups of students and the class as a whole. For many of us, talking is easy, but really listening to is more difficult. Listening requires us to actively reflect on what the speaker says and does. It sends the messages, "I care about you" and "You are important to me," sometimes more strongly than simply saying them.

While developing relationships and bonding with all of our students is key to their achievement, this is perhaps even truer for the student from poverty. Educational professional Ruby Payne discusses this in her book, *A Framework for Understanding Poverty* (aha! Process, Inc., 2001). She writes, "When students who have been in poverty (and have successfully made it into middle class) are asked how they made the journey, the answer nine times out of ten has to do with a relationship—a teacher, counselor, or coach who made a suggestion or took an interest in them as individuals" (143).

Keeping your classroom student-centered means that you find ways to make students matter when they are there. It is sending them the message that the classroom is not the same when they are gone and that you value their relationship with you. Each Friday, the students in Susan's class fill out exit cards sharing their reflections on the week and their learning. Leanna, a child of poverty, wrote Susan a card shortly after entering the class that indicated she finally felt she was part of a community. She wrote, "I [sic] proud to have you in my life I do not know what I would do if you was [sic] not here. Love, Leanna."

Data-Driven Classrooms

There is a current trend in education to use data to make informed instructional decisions in the classroom. We agree that for too long, we as teachers (and particularly elementary teachers) were often teaching based on programs, our own likes, and/or current philosophical trends. Rarely did student needs impact what we did in the classroom. The shift to being more focused on the use of classroom data is positive. But there is a danger, too. Data can sometimes make us very narrow-minded. We have to know that each piece of data that is collected on a student gives us a glimpse into who they are and what they know, but it is also a reminder that we have to reflect on the whole child.

With the emergence of high-stakes standardized tests in all states, the reality is that we often have a knee-jerk reaction when the scores arrive. It's our nature to want to "fix-up" anything that seems wrong or out of place. In Susan's district this year, there was a meeting of the data coaches and the district test coordinator before the arrival of scores. The coaches were told to "suspend judgment." Note that they were not told *Don't* judge." In fact, the key word here is "suspend." Rather than looking for things that needed to be fixed right away and making rash decisions, coaches were reminded that they needed to look deeper and try to see the whole picture. This means looking at multiple sources of data, both formal and informal, and *then* planning for instruction.

Data coach Debra Voege gives this example: When scores come back and a child demonstrates weakness in an area, we tend to cry out "Remediate!" It would be like a child who is weak in reference skills, for example, being put in a remedial class on using reference materials until he or she knows that skill. It's so much more than that. Certainly that student may need instruction in reference skills. But it may be as simple as providing vocabulary instruction, building background knowledge for different reference materials, or giving the student some real-world examples and applications for using reference skills. Our instinct should be to ask, "What is the next step I need to take with this student to move him or her forward in literacy acquisition?"

Mellissa says "Every number on a data sheet has a story to tell." Excellent classroom teachers will take the time to excavate the information. Then they use that information and look at other pieces of information before making instructional decisions. When we look at the whole picture, think about what the child knows and can do, and then plan for instruction, our classrooms become authentic and rich, "data-driven" learning environments.

Finding a Balance

The implications of balanced teaching and learning are many in the primary classroom. Certainly there must be an instructional focus on phonemic awareness, phonics, vocabulary development, fluency, and comprehension. Proficiency in these five areas helps students seek meaning in text. Seeking meaning in reading and writing is the thread that weaves these literacy strands together.

We must also balance our instructional delivery that happens daily in the classroom. This includes modeled, shared, and guided practice as well as independent opportunities to demonstrate understanding. These are the essential components of learning. All learning requires support that will eventually lead to independence.

Gradual Release of Responsibility

Learning anything new, no matter what it is, has some common components. As we wrote this book, Susan's oldest son Daniel was learning to drive. This was a learning experience both for the parents and the student! Daniel watched his parents drive for a very long time prior to getting his permit. However, this model wasn't effective until it became relevant to him. Since getting his learner's permit, he has watched the modeling with a more critical and dissecting eye. Initially, he only drove in parking lots. This was more of a guided practice where he took over more and more responsibility. Within the confines of guidance comes a wide range of responsibility. The adults had to coach him less and less as he became more and more independent. Eventually, he was completely on his own on the road. This example is similar to P. David Pearson's Gradual Release of Responsibility model (Pearson and Gallagher, 1983).

In your classroom, you model skills and strategies that you want your students to know. Then you practice these with them, gradually releasing them to practice the tasks with less and less support and feedback from you. This is shared practice. Then, you allow students to practice with only necessary guidance from you. Finally, you expect students to apply what they have learned to new situations. The reader's and writer's workshops are based on this concept of modeled, shared, guided, and independent practice.

Components of Reader's Workshop	Components of Writer's Workshop
Read Aloud: Reading aloud daily models oral fluency and builds listening comprehension. As the model, you read *to* the students "acting as the author and the reader" (Mooney, 1990). They are released from the responsibility of concentrating on the mechanics of reading and are free to enjoy the text. Responsibility level: Teacher	**Modeled Writing:** Modeled writing is a time for students to watch and listen as you think, talk, and write about any topic. As you write, think aloud about strategies, conventions, ideas, and language. This instructional opportunity places you, the teacher, in the role of an author. *You* hold the pen as *you* write about *your* ideas. Responsibility level: Teacher
Shared Reading: Shared reading mirrors the bedtime story situation when the reader and the child interact with print (Holdaway, 1979). In the classroom, you read *with* the students as they interact with a variety of genres, such as poetry, fiction, and informational text (Mooney, 1990). This support allows active participation as you explicitly teach and model strategies for reading. Students have visual access to the text in the form of Big Books, charts, overhead transparencies, and so on. Responsibility level: Teacher and students	**Shared Writing:** Shared writing encourages you and the students to collaborate on a piece of writing. Together, you negotiate ideas, language, and conventions as you compose the text. *You* hold the pen and record contributions. **Interactive Writing:** During interactive writing, all the elements of shared writing are present except for one: You now *sha*re the pen with the students. Students can help you write a letter, word, or sentence depending upon their level. Responsibility level: Teacher and students
Guided Reading: Guided reading provides a small group of students with the opportunity to talk, think, and question their way through text (Mooney, 1990). Each student holds a copy of the text, and the reading is done *by* the students as the teacher talks *with* the members of the group. Your role is to ensure an appropriate match between the students and the text by determining the supports and challenges within the text and the needs of the readers. Responsibility Level: Students with teacher as Coach	**Guided Writing:** Guided writing immediately follows the whole-group lesson. This is the time for students to try out the skills and strategies you have modeled. As students write, you provide support and guidance through individual or small-group conferences. The writing is often shorter pieces where students practice developing organization, voice, word choice, sentence fluency, and conventions. Students can compose new pieces or practice revision. Responsibility Level: Students with teacher as coach
Independent Reading: Students self-select texts that they can read on their own. This can be based on interest as well as level. The reading occurs completely *by* the students. This offers an opportunity for fluency-building and deeper understanding. A rich independent reading program is supported by a well-stocked Classroom Library. Responsibility Level: Student	**Independent Writing:** Independent writing allows students to experiment, gain fluency, and write freely. Sources of support, such as word lists, word walls, and dictionaries, should be present for student use. Students should be explicitly taught when and how to use the resources in the room to assist them during this time. Responsibility Level: Student

We believe that meaningful literacy centers provide an opportunity for students to practice and apply the skills and strategies that you teach in your modeled, shared, and guided lessons. Well-constructed literacy centers also lead students to develop new skills and strategies on their own through natural exploration.

How to Use This Book

This book is divided into two parts. The remainder of Part One will help you as you are setting up or rethinking your center time. You will find tips for effective center use in the classroom, learn how to connect centers to your curriculum standards, and hear from teachers and students about center use.

Part Two is divided into eight sections that detail balanced literacy lesson plans and their corresponding centers. Each section focuses on a specific reading or writing strategy (four of each) and starts with a table listing the four Literacy Connection Planners outlined in the section. A planner is composed of a corresponding mini-lesson, center, and activity. These planners are designed to help you connect centers directly to your Reader's and Writer's Workshop instruction. Each Literacy Connection Planner includes a note-taking section so that you can personalize your lessons and differentiate instruction for your students. You will find many ideas for materials and activities to maximize center use.

For those of you who would like some quick center ideas to implement into your classroom tomorrow, you will find a helpful Center Index in the Teacher Resources on page 191.

If you are just beginning to implement literacy centers in your classroom, we suggest you read "A Quick-Start Guide to Literacy Centers," originally published in *Primary Literacy Centers* and located in the Teacher Resources section at the end of this book.

In *Primary Literacy Centers*, we used the following "STICK" acronym to implement centers in the classroom:

Strategy immersion in centers
Tools that target all learners
Increase time in text
Choice, not chaos
Keys to success

While we still believe these are critical to center set-up, we have decided to change some of this acronym for the purposes of this book. These changes reflect our ongoing learning as teachers. They also will be a way for you to think more deeply about literacy center implementation in your own classroom.

Strategy Teaching Cycle
Transitioning readers from emergent to fluent
Interacting as a learning community
Content, conversations, and comprehension
Keeping the focus

Chapter One
Center Basics

In Regie Routman's book, *Reading Essentials: The Specifics You Need to Teach Reading Well* (Heinemann, 2003), she writes: "Centers have become another orthodoxy: teachers feel they have to have them for management and learning. In some places, "literacy centers" are actually mandated. If "centers"—structured activities for small groups of students while the teacher is meeting with a guided reading group—are worthwhile, have a meaningful purpose and are contributing to reading achievement and enjoyment, great. If not, rethink how you and your students have been spending your time" (163).

This is certainly a thought-provoking statement with which we agree. Doing a center for the sake of saying that you are doing a center is neither productive nor effective and will not produce lasting results. Further, it will not have an effect on the literacy acquisition of your students. It is critical that you know your students and your instructional learning goals as you set up and design meaningful literacy activities in your classroom.

What's in a Name?

Many teachers are hung up on the word "centers." They envision a place where chaos abounds and work quality is compromised. Whether you call it a literacy club, a work station, a learning opportunity, workjobs, or anything else, we believe that all independent literacy activities must have some shared qualities. For the purposes of this book, we will use the word "centers." It is our goal to help you make your centers more meaningful and relevant to your learners. We believe a literacy center must:

- Invite students to practice and apply strategies that have been taught and modeled in shared and guided literacy lessons
- Promote reading, writing, speaking, listening, and viewing
- Allow students to manipulate language in both oral and written forms
- Engage the learner through interaction
- Expose students to a variety of text
- Provide open-ended activities for students
- Enable the teacher to assess and evaluate the students' use of literacy strategies
- Encourage opportunities for safe, meaningful practice
- Scaffold learning for students while also providing opportunities for them to acquire new literacy skills and strategies

Remember, what's worked in the past may need to change when you get a new group of students. Each year, you will need to rethink your purpose and priorities as you plan for meaningful literacy center practice in your classroom. For more information on rethinking centers, see Chapter 6: "K—Keeping the Focus" in this book.

A Guide to Getting Started

Here are some questions and answers to consider before you start your centers:

Why do I want to implement centers in my classroom?

If your answer is not a resounding "So my students can practice and apply their literacy skills and strategies," then you need to rethink your "why." If you want center time to be filled with depth and complexity, then you must set your centers up to invite student inquiry as well as the practice and application of skills.

Think about how you learn best. Very few of us would honestly say we learn by listening to lecture delivery. Learners learn by doing. Literacy acquisition is a social process. It requires talking, thinking, sharing, and listening to and with others. Centers provide the perfect opportunity for hands-on, interactive learning in your classroom.

Who will be doing the most work?

Think about it. Who will do the most work at this center—you or your students? If you are spending an inordinate amount of time thinking up, planning for, and implementing centers—stop! All centers in your classroom should have one purpose. They must be set up so that the students are doing most of the work in them. If you spend your time making a cute game to go into the word work center and your kids are finished with it in five minutes, it's probably not worth your time or effort—and it is probably not extending their skills and strategies. If, however, your word work center is inviting kids to delve into word building and word meanings, then they are doing the most work. The centers in this book are designed to help you work smarter, not harder.

What do I want my kids to do when they are in the centers and not with me?

OK, truth be told, many of us would answer this question with "Be quiet so I can teach a small group!" It really is more than that though. The goal of highly-effective teachers is to have students engaged in meaningful literacy activities so that we can teach small groups and maximize the learning of all students in the classroom community. The literacy center time should be filled with opportunities for students to practice and extend their reading, writing, speaking, listening, and viewing skills and strategies.

Where will I put each center?

When we are out talking to teachers about implementing centers, the complaint we hear the most is "I don't have space!" Sometimes you have to be creative. We truly find that when space is the issue, "necessity is the mother of invention." Some of the most creative centers we have seen have been in small spaces. One teacher uses tubs and small baskets and converts student desks into centers during the center time. Another one uses large envelopes that the student takes to his or her desk to complete the center activity. If space is an issue for you, think about taking a walk through your building and seeing what other teachers are doing. Very often, the best solutions are right next door and we are missing them! For more ideas on where and how to set up centers, see "A Quick-Start Guide to Literacy Centers" on page 159 in the Teacher Resources.

When will center time be implemented in my day?

Center time usually begins during the guided reading or small group portion of the language arts block. This is usually forty to sixty minutes of time each day. Students are then pulled from centers for a small-group guided reading or a strategy-focus lesson. The important thing to keep in mind is consistency. Your students want to know what is happening and when it will happen. When you set up centers as an ongoing routine, you will foster the independence and the interdependence your students need so that you can easily teach your small groups.

How will I keep centers updated and engaging for my students?

Much of this book deals with how to keep centers engaging for your students. When the "how-to" of each center stays the same, students will know the routine. There is a danger, however, of students losing their interest in this type of center. We find the simplest thing can freshen up a center. For example, add highlighters to the Writing Center, new puppets to the Classroom Library, and brightly-colored paper or other simple art materials to the Literature Response Center. These simple additions will re-engage students as they work in your centers each day.

Steps to Success

1. Set up your space.

Decide where the center will be housed. Remember, if you find that a center doesn't work in a specific space, you may need to move it.

Here are some center "housing" suggestions:
- Dedicated desk or table
- Baskets or tubs that move to student workspace
- Hula hoops on the floor to define a space
- Folder or envelope to take the centers to a desk
- Small gift bags or lunch boxes to house center materials
- Project display boards that can be taken out for center time and tucked away at other times
- Gift bags with themes

Tip: Make sure your noisiest centers and centers that require a lot of movement are not too close to your guided reading area. This allows you to focus on the instruction in your small group. However, make sure you have a clear view of all learning areas in your classroom.

2. Hold a class meeting.

Before implementing a center, hold a class meeting in or near the center space. Bring students together and role-play how the center will be set up and used. Be sure and ask students for their ideas about how this space should be used. They often have the best ideas just waiting to be implemented! Be prepared to hold class meetings throughout the year as you add new materials and/or need to revisit procedures and routines.

3. Set a purpose for the center.

After you demonstrate the use of materials in the center, explain to students what they will learn and practice when they are there. For older students, you may want to write the purpose on a sentence strip. For example: "This center will help me practice and improve _____." For younger students, you may have to revisit a center occasionally to remind students why they are doing it.

Tip: At the end of the week, have students identify and discuss in their writing journal one center they used. They can reflect on how the activities in that center helped them become a better reader or writer. Post some of these responses in appropriate centers. A "Center Learning Reflection Log" is included in the Teacher Resources on page 180.

4. Identify the materials to be used.

Don't expect your students to automatically know how much tape to pull off the roll, how many staples they need to make a book, and/or what to do when the pencil breaks. Discuss each piece of material that will be housed in the center. Clearly label baskets so students know where things belong. Invite students to model appropriate use of all center materials prior to letting them use the center independently. When center materials are misused throughout the year—that is a sign that it is time for another class meeting.

5. Fill out a "Looks Like/Sounds Like" chart.

We find it is helpful to fill out a "Looks Like/Sounds Like" chart (see the Teacher Resources on page 181). Together, students can brainstorm words and phrases to show what should be happening when they are present in the center. Explain that this chart will be posted to remind everyone of the appropriate uses of the center materials and of proper center behavior.

For emergent learners, take photographs of students in the center modeling what should be happening there. For example, if the center is a place where students should talk quietly to one another, have two students sit next to each other and talk. Take their picture for the "Sounds

Like" side of the chart. If there are specific storage containers or materials to be used at the center, take a picture and put it on the "Looks Like" side of the chart. Have students dictate the words to label the photos and attach them to the "Looks Like/Sounds Like" chart.

6. Role-play procedures and routines.

It is said, "If you want to learn something, teach it." Have your students teach others how to use the centers in your classroom. Additionally, have students practice what to do when they are called for small group and how they will return to the centers at the end of small group.

Any time you get a new student, appoint some "student teachers" to acquaint him or her with each one of your classroom centers.

7. Plan storage for completed products.

Not all centers will have products, but in those that do, you will need to plan where completed work will be stored. Some teachers keep a "finished" basket at the center in which students can insert their completed work. Others give each student a pocket folder to keep all of the week's completed work. Make sure your students know and understand your plan for work they have finished.

8. Practice using each center with a small group first.

Before releasing an entire class of students to the centers, try out one with a few students. While the class is working on a whole-group activity, allow a small group to try out the center activities in the designated area. This allows you to provide immediate feedback and make quick adjustments as necessary. This is especially important with a group of students who are entirely new to centers and/or are more challenging to manage. Remember that even those students who have done centers in another classroom will need to practice following your procedures and expectations.

9. Gradually add another center.

You can add the next center using steps one through eight. After you have introduced three or more centers, you can help students begin to understand their center rotations. This entire process usually takes three to four weeks. Remember that the time you invest in the beginning will save you time later on in the year.

When Centers Break Down

Are all of your markers dry and capless? Are books strewn all over the place? Has the class pet disappeared? Are the glue lids full of dried glue? Sometimes center use breaks down and the center becomes ineffective. When this happens, don't get discouraged. Ask yourself why and then develop a plan to fix it.

Ask yourself the following questions:

- What is the problem?
- Is the problem with the center or an activity within the center?
- Are there too many activities in the center? Or not enough?
- What is the real purpose of this center and/or activity?
- What are some possible solutions?

Don't hesitate to hold a class meeting in the center, revisit the "Looks Like/Sounds Like" chart, and ask students for their solutions. This sends a very important message to your students. They will know that they are an important part of the planning and learning that happens in your room.

When you take the time to set up your centers well, you and your students will find that deeper, more meaningful literacy acquisition will take place.

Chapter Two
S—Strategy Teaching Cycle

The beating heart provides a good visual metaphor for instructional delivery in classrooms, where the balance between modeling and instruction and guided practice pulses evenly back and forth. Gathering kids in front for instruction, releasing them to practice, and then bringing them back to share their thinking represents the steady flow that is at the heart of effective teaching and learning.

Stephanie Harvey and Anne Goudvis, *Strategies That Work: Teaching Comprehension to Enhance Understanding* (31)

As this book has developed, many changes have taken place in American education. With the emphasis on high-stakes test performance, we find many teachers are abandoning the meaningful literacy experiences that literacy centers can provide. They are exchanging them for test-preparation workbooks and worksheets, whole-class drills, and isolated skill focus. When we enter classrooms, we often find ourselves asking, "How can we help students prepare for high-stakes test-taking in the context of authentic reading and writing experiences?" Teachers tell us they don't have time to do literacy centers. We would argue you don't have time NOT to do literacy centers. The literacy center experience must be a natural extension of your classroom teaching. It is allowing students the opportunity to put into practice the skills and strategies you teach and model every day.

There is a resurgence of "deficit model teaching" in America's classrooms. This is when we assess to find out what children don't know, or their deficiencies, and then teach it until we think they should know it. Finally, they are tested to see if they "got it." The tragedy is this: when students don't get it, many teachers feel pressured to limit their teaching to only the deficiencies, thus narrowing the curriculum and leaving the struggling learner feeling unaccomplished and further behind.

Of course teachers should assess and be keenly aware of what students need to learn. In fact, as discussed in the introduction, we believe data-driven instruction is critical if we are to move students forward in their thinking and learning. We are suggesting that, in addition to knowing a student's deficiencies, we must be aware of what our students know and can do. When we are aware of both proficiencies and deficiencies, then we can learn from and teach the whole child.

The centers in this book will help students as they work to integrate new knowledge with what they already know. They must work with materials, concepts, and processes that are familiar to them. This familiarity invites the learner to take the risk of learning new material. It's like the child who learns to ride a two-wheel bike. She must be comfortable with the training wheels first before she is willing to take the risk required to balance on the two-wheeler. When our centers are meaningful, they include materials that students know and can use while also providing them the time and opportunity to take the next step in their literacy journey. As students work in the known, they can begin to acquire the new. In her book, *Reading Recovery: A Guidebook for Teachers in Training,* Marie Clay notes: "The most important reason for roaming around the known is that it requires the teacher to stop teaching from her preconceived ideas. She has to work from the child's responses." (p. 13).

Centers with a Purpose

Literacy instruction is becoming the focal point of primary classrooms throughout the country. We know that young children need to read and write a lot in order to become fluent and independent readers and writers. With the development of the Reading First legislation (Title I, Part B, Subpart 1, of the No Child Left Behind Act), it is imperative that students have systematic and explicit language arts instruction in all aspects of reading and writing. One very important component of systematic instruction is practice and application. If we spend our time teaching students skills and strategies but don't give them the opportunity for authentic practice, then our instruction will not have a long-lasting impact on their literacy development.

In *Primary Literacy Centers*, we suggested that teachers need to know and understand the concept of balanced literacy prior to implementing centers. It is important that the classroom environment is set up in such a way that there are ample modeled, shared, and guided lessons prior to asking students to perform or practice in a center. See page 18 of this book for more information about the components of balanced literacy.

The Strategy Teaching Cycle

It is clear that connections must be made between data and assessment, lesson planning, implementation, and practice. We call this the Strategy Teaching Cycle (*Primary Literacy Centers,* Maupin House, 2001). As we reflected on trends in education and discussed the relevance of this cycle, we realized that it reflects good teaching. Therefore, we felt it was important to reiterate in this book.

When a teacher can articulate where he or she is in the cycle of strategy teaching and why he or she is there, then quality teaching and learning can happen in the classroom .

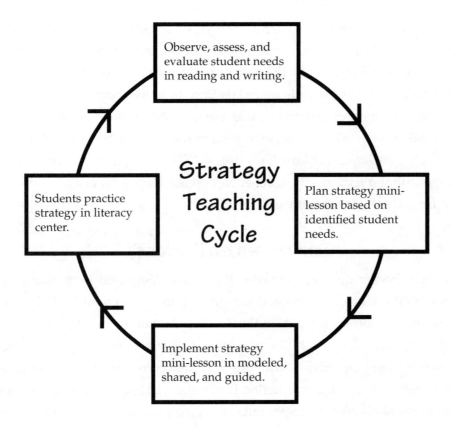

Observe, assess, and evaluate student needs in reading and writing.

Strategy Teaching Cycle

Plan strategy mini-lesson based on identified student needs.

Students practice strategy in literacy center.

Implement strategy mini-lesson in modeled, shared, and guided.

Understand the Skills and Strategies

Know your grade-level expectations. Before you jump into the act of strategy teaching, it is critical that you are aware of the expectations, skills, strategies, and benchmarks that your state or district has defined for your grade. These are often distributed to teachers via the district office, Internet, or State Department of Education. It is no longer acceptable for a highly-qualified educator to open to the next lesson in a teacher's guide and simply teach it because it is there. All teaching and learning that takes place in the classroom should be designed to move students further along the literacy continuum. Table I, excerpted from *Primary Literacy Centers*, lists eight reading and writing strategies. Each strategy definition includes the NCTE/IRA Standard Correlations. These standards are foundational to most district or state benchmarks throughout the country.

Reading Strategies	Writing Strategies
Strategies for Comprehension - readers construct meaning from a variety of text. • using prior knowledge to interact with text • confirming/revising predictions about text • rereading to self-monitor for comprehension • summarizing information from text (NCTE/IRA Standard 3)	**Strategies for Communicating a Message** - writers construct text for a variety of purposes. • selecting an appropriate form of writing with an audience in mind • checking for meaning using self-monitoring strategies (rereading, revising for understanding) (NCTE/IRA Standard 5)
Strategies for Learning and Using Words - readers use their understanding of word identification and meaning during text interaction. • using sound/symbol relationships to identify new words • using word families/word patterns to identify new words • using context cues or word structures to construct meaning • using resources and references to build vocabulary (dictionary, thesaurus, word wall, peers, etc.) (NCTE/IRA Standard 3)	**Strategies for Word Choice** - writers use their understanding of words and their meaning to make effective word choices. • choosing clear and specific words to convey meaning to an audience • engaging the reader using descriptive details • using models of literature as a source for understanding word choice • revising word choice to build understanding for the reader (NCTE/IRA Standard 4)
Strategies for Finding Information - readers gather, evaluate, and synthesize data from a variety of sources. • selecting and organizing information from text • using textual information to support an answer (NCTE/IRA Standard 7)	**Strategies for Using Information** - writers communicate their discoveries for a variety of purposes and audiences. • organizing information to present to an audience • recording observations using descriptive details (NCTE/IRA Standard 7)
Strategies for Building Fluency and Independence - readers self-select appropriate text and read for a variety of purposes. • attending to punctuation and reading in whole phrases rather than word by word • reading with expression and intonation • reinforcing sentence syntax by murmur reading (NCTE/IRA Standard 12)	**Strategies for Building Fluency and Independence** - writers self-select topics and write for a variety of purposes. • using prior knowledge of the topic to write with fluency • making choices regarding publication • reinforcing sentence syntax using edit-by-ear technique (NCTE/IRA Standard 12)

Many school districts and state departments of education have identified expectations or standards for the language arts based on the NCTE/IRA standards. We encourage you to check your local district or state department expectations and/or standards. Once you identify them, then you are ready to begin the Strategy Teaching Cycle.

Once you have an understanding of what you are expected to teach, you can begin implementing the Strategy Teaching Cycle as explained in this chapter.

Observe, Assess, and Evaluate

There are many opportunities to observe, assess, and evaluate student learning throughout the day. Your records are evidence of student performance. They are often used to determine student grades for progress reports and to conference with parents, but they also need to be a regular part of planning for instruction. The teacher who is implementing strategy teaching uses this information to set up reading groups, select appropriate instructional materials, and make changes in the classroom as necessary.

Following is a chart that illustrates some of the assessment opportunities that may occur during each component of the balanced literacy framework. We know that you already have many assessment tools in your classroom. This list is simply designed to help you think beyond your current practice. Use the lines in each box to add to and personalize this chart.

Balanced Literacy Experiences	Assessment Opportunities
Modeled	Class discussions, retelling charts, story mapping, _____ _____ _____
Shared	Schema charts, making connections, student-lead reading, locating information in text, class discussions, _____ _____ _____
Guided	Oral reading records, fluency checks, oral and written retellings, anecdotal records, writing samples, group and individual discussions, _____ _____ _____
Independent	Response journals, reading logs, dialogue journals, teacher-student conferencing, _____ _____ _____

These assessment opportunities provide you with information about what students know and can do, as well as areas of need. It is important to plan instruction with both in mind.

Remember, we cannot always be focused on the deficit model of teaching and learning where we try to fill in the gaps for our students. We must also think about how to extend and enrich students knowledge as we help them become lifelong learners.

From the Classroom: *When Julie Collins looked extensively at her first-grade students' individual reading logs, she noticed that most students were selecting and reading a wealth of fiction books during independent reading. She noted that most of her students were not selecting informational texts for their independent reading. Upon further reflection, Julie determined that most of her read-alouds were conducted using her own favorite fictional stories. In an effort to introduce these young students to the joy of reading informational text and to integrate a science unit on life cycles, she began reading classroom newsmagazines as well as other relevant pieces of informational text during her daily read-aloud.*

Plan Targeted Mini-Lessons

After you have collected individual and group data on your students through your assessments and observations, plan the mini-lesson by asking yourself the following questions:

- What trends or patterns do I see in the data?
- Is the trend or pattern an individual, small-group, or whole-class need?
- What will help move my students' literacy learning forward?
- What resources do I have to teach this skill or strategy?
- Should this lesson be delivered in a modeled, shared, or guided format?

Strategy Teaching Cycle

Observe, assess and evaluate student needs in reading and writing.

Plan strategy mini-lesson based on identified student needs.

Implement strategy mini-lesson in modeled, shared and guided experiences.

Students practice strategy in literacy center.

From the Classroom: *To further enhance this immersion in information and to complement a unit on life cycles, Julie selected the book* Busy as a Bee *by Melvin Berger (Newbridge Educational Publishing, 1995). She planned to use this book over time in her daily shared reading sessions to help students notice features of informational text, develop vocabulary concepts, and learn to organize and present information to an audience. To accomplish this final goal, she planned to take the book from shared reading to the shared writing portion of her literacy block.*

Implement Strategy Mini-Lessons

After you have assessed and planned, you are ready to deliver the strategy mini-lesson. It is important that you remain aware of your focus during the instructional delivery while also being responsive to student reactions and feedback. Sometimes, in an effort to deliver a "flawless lesson," we miss important "teachable moments." If your focus is student-centered, then you won't be afraid to follow the ebb and flow of thoughts and ideas generated by your community of learners. While there are moments that we want to follow a student's thought or idea, we must also stay aware of our teaching purpose and the goals for all our learners. Let these moments drive your decisions for later instruction as you continue the Strategy Teaching Cycle in your classroom.

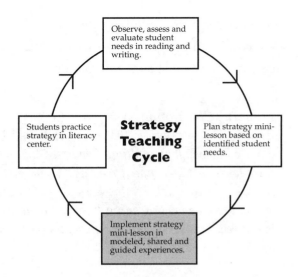

From Susan: *One teacher that I know keeps a chart on her board titled, "Things we want to learn about..." When a student comes up with an idea that seems "off track" during a lesson, she writes it directly on the chart to remind them to visit the thought or idea at a more appropriate time. This shows her students she values their thinking and learning while keeping her instructional momentum going.*

From the Classroom: *As Julie again presented the book* Busy as a Bee *to her students during a shared-writing lesson, she announced that many times readers like to write about their reading for another audience. She explained that information is often shared in a written report, but it could also be shared in a totally different way like a song or a poem. At this point, she asked her readers to think like writers and share how they would like to present their information. Because this class had spent extensive time enjoying poetry, they chose to write a poem together.*

Practice and Application in Literacy Centers

Traditionally, teachers have followed the "assess—teach—test—reteach and/or enrich" model of teaching. The Strategy Teaching Cycle is not very different from this traditional model except for this one component: practice and apply in literacy centers. In many ways, leaving the practice and application out is like asking a young musician to play his instrument in a performance without any rehearsal. We are often ready to test what hasn't been sufficiently honed and practiced. As stated in Chapter 1, literacy centers must "invite students to practice and apply strategies that have been taught and modeled in shared and guided literacy lessons."

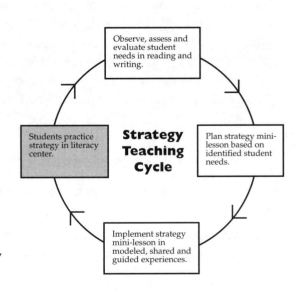

There are many ways to facilitate this practice and application in your classroom. Remember that you will not always be able to integrate material from a lesson into every one of your classroom centers. Look for those natural connections between instruction and practice. Keep the connections and practice meaningful and authentic. Throughout this book, we will share many ideas with you. You, of course, know your students best and must think about what will work in your classroom. We encourage you to make notes and personalize this information for yourself as you read.

From the Classroom: After Julie's class spent time participating in read-aloud, shared reading, and shared writing with informational text, she integrated many aspects of these lessons into her classroom literacy centers. Following is a list of the centers and activities that she was able to use to enrich and extend her lessons.

Centers	Connection
Classroom Library	Big Book and read-alouds are placed in this center for students to revisit either independently or with a partner.
Read the Room	The class-created chart poem "I Like Bees" is posted clearly in the classroom along with a variety of pointers for students to practice reading.
Research	Photos of bees are displayed and labeled. Students practice making their own diagrams of bees and labeling parts.
Writing	A bee vocabulary chart is posted, and students are encouraged to write about what they learned about bees as they visit this center.

Strategy Teaching Builds a Rich Literacy Context for Learning

Julie Collins' focused instruction built a rich literacy context for students to learn in her classroom. They used materials that were familiar while also developing important new skills and strategies. The literacy experiences they had during modeled, guided, and shared reading and writing were further developed in their literacy centers. Using this model, students begin to take ownership of their own learning. Meaningful teaching and learning are a natural part of the strategy teaching classroom. The resulting culture is one where rich literacy experiences take place every day.

The Literacy Connection Planners found in Part Two of this book follow the organization of the Strategy Teaching Cycle introduced in this chapter. The section is divided into the eight reading and writing strategies from the table on page 17. As a result of your assessments, you can locate the strategy lessons that will best meet the needs of your students and implement them in your classroom. Each Literacy Connection Planner includes a literacy center suggestion to give students practice and application opportunities. If your centers are instructionally sound (directly connected to your assessments and instruction), it's easy to justify the amount of time you spend preparing them and the amount of time your students spend using them.

Chapter Three
T—Transitioning Readers from Emergent to Fluent

Kids not only need to read a lot, but they also need lots of books they can read right at their fingertips. They also need access to books that entice them to reading. Schools can foster wider reading by creating school and classroom collections that provide a rich and wide array of appropriate books and magazines and by providing time every day for children to actually sit and read.

Dr. Richard Allington, *What Really Matters for Struggling Readers: Designing Research-Based Programs* (68)

Your classrooms are rich communities of learners, diverse in student levels and experiences. A big question teachers often ask us at workshops is "How do I make sure I am meeting all levels of learners through my literacy centers?" No matter if you teach in a self-contained, multi-age, or departmentalized classroom, your students are not all at the same level of development. Nor do they have the same interests. It is crucial to begin the year by learning as much as you can about the students you teach. You can gather this information through interest inventories, writing samples, conferencing, and so on. As with any good instructional practice, you assess the students to find their strengths and areas of need as you plan for instruction. But how will this impact your literacy centers?

Understanding Characteristics of Readers and Writers

As you group for literacy centers, we suggest you maintain heterogeneous groups of students. This creates a support system for struggling students as well as challenging opportunities for more proficient readers. Center activities need to be open-ended to allow for these differences. Here are a few questions to keep in mind as you prepare your literacy centers:

- What types of readers and writers do I have in my classroom this year?
- What types of activities do emergent, early, and fluent readers need?
- How will the centers look at the beginning of the year?
- As my instruction changes, how will this impact my centers over time?

A young reader uses a magnifying glass to focus on specific parts of text.

The following descriptions are broad, detailed characteristics of readers and writers. Use this information as you consider ways to make centers open-ended and multi-level.

Emergent readers and writers are learning about print concepts in reading and writing. They are becoming aware that print carries a message and that letters have names. They are beginning to connect sounds to these symbols. Emergent readers need books with a strong text-picture match and repetitive and predictable language patterns that reflect the way they naturally speak. Their writing may begin with drawings, scribbles, strands of letters, beginning sounds, and so on. Many times they can even read what they write. They like to write about topics they have personally experienced.

Early readers and writers are beginning to pay more attention to the text than the pictures. They use their background knowledge to comprehend what they are reading. Text gradually becomes more difficult and readers begin to use strategies to "solve" words while maintaining meaning. They are developing a bank of high-frequency words to use in reading and writing. They write simple sentences and approximate spelling. These writers also are learning to use resources for spelling, such as word walls, charts, and word lists.

Fluent readers and writers are becoming more proficient in using strategies for comprehension and word solving. They are beginning to use "fix-up" strategies when meaning breaks down. They still benefit from practice with easier texts to develop oral fluency and deepen comprehension. They are reading from a variety of genres as texts become increasingly longer and more difficult. Their reading may influence their writing through topic selection, word choice, and sentence structure. As writers, they are beginning to elaborate on ideas and use their voice in their writing.

Incorporating Different Levels in Literacy Centers

The following chart illustrates how literacy centers can serve many levels of students. The information reflected in the chart is designed to give you additional ideas for each center while also providing you with an opportunity to observe how the activities transition over time. For example, two students may be visiting the Classroom Library at the same time. One student may be rereading a familiar text and creating props for a retelling while the other student is writing a recommendation to the class about her book.

		Literacy Centers across Levels	
Types of Centers	**Emergent Readers and Writers**	**Early Readers and Writers**	**Fluent Readers and Writers**
Classroom Library	• Reread favorite read-alouds and Big Books. • Read to a puppet or buddy. • Add props for retelling.	• Revisit favorite read-alouds and Big Books for specific purposes. • Reread favorite authors and titles to build fluency and comprehension.	• Read independent materials. • Create a recommendation board or chart for students to share favorite books. • Have students join in-class "book clubs" to talk about books they are reading.
Listening	• Ask school personnel or parents to record a book on tape. Organize each tape and book set in a zipper storage bag. • Record the class reading its favorite Big Book aloud. Place the text and tape at this center.	• Provide paper and markers for students to respond to what they liked best about the book they just heard. • Help students create a chart titled "You've got to hear this book!" to display at the center.	• After listening to a selection on tape, have students write a short summary of the text. • Create a class rubric for what makes a quality book-on- tape. After listening to a selection, have students rate the tape.
Literature Response	• Model **one** response stem such as: *I notice…* *I think…* *I like…* • Provide paper for students to draw their responses.	• Begin an "I learned…" page in a reader's response notebook. Have students select a familiar informational text and write what they learned about the topic.	• Return to a prediction chart created by the class before reading a story. At the center, have students write a response about their prediction and how the story actually turned out.
Poetry	• Write the words to familiar songs, poems, and nursery rhymes on charts for readers to point to as they read. • Have students find rhyming words.	• Type the words to a familiar poem or song and have students place in a poetry journal. They can highlight words they already know or find interesting.	• Model how to make personal connections. As students collect poems in their poetry notebooks, have them write a connection to a particular poem.
Research	• Display an informational Big Book or photographs about a familiar topic and have students draw and write what they know about the topic.	• Model how to write an "I wonder…" statement before reading. • Provide informational books about a familiar topic, and have students write "I wonder…" statements.	• Have students select an informational magazine such as *Ranger Rick* or *Zoobooks* to research a topic. • Copy an article and have students highlight important information and report on what they learned.
Word Work	• Place a student name chart in the Word Work center. Glue a photo of each child next to their name. • Create a name puzzle center by writing the students' names on an envelope. Enclose a set of cut-up letters in the envelope for students to name-build.	• Have students find an anchor word on the word wall such as "at" (place a star next to these words). Students then create a list of words that can be made using the anchor word: *at* *cat* *sat* *that*	• Use a list of class names to highlight specific word patterns (silent letters, consonant digraphs, etc.). • Locate bolded or italicized words in an informational text. Use context clues to determine meaning. • Add new words to a personal word wall or dictionary for writing.
Writing	• Keep a picture file at the center for self-selected writing. This helps them when they cannot generate their own topic. • Place alphabet strips at students' eye level instead of high above bulletin boards to ensure easy access.	• Invite students to return to an earlier journal entry and expand the idea at the Writing Center. • Use a variety of resources during center time such as high-frequency word walls, name word walls, theme word charts, etc.	• "Borrow from the experts" by using real books to serve as models for lead statements, word choice, sentence variety, elaboration, etc. • Write to authors and share what students like best about their books and craft of writing.

Designing Open-Ended Responses

A center is open-ended if it

- invites students to reuse it for a variety of purposes,
- can be used with a variety of texts, and
- includes materials for students to "dig deeper" into their learning.

The "Literacy Response Chart" on the following page is another way to make literacy centers meaningful, open-ended, and multi-level. Students can respond to a text they have heard or read. The responses illustrated on the left side of the matrix are appropriate for informational text while the responses on the right are better suited for literary text. To make the activities more meaningful, place copies of the text in the center and have students return to the text to locate information to support their responses. Explanations of these responses are on the "Literatacy Response Chart with Explanations" located in the Teacher Resources on page 188.

From Mellissa: One of the teachers in our district expanded the idea of the "Literacy Response Chart" on a large bulletin board. She begins the year with the bulletin board empty except for gridlines. She introduces each of the literature responses one at a time to the whole class. She demonstrates how to use the materials and what a quality response looks like. If the response is one that she wants her students to use in her classroom during the year, she adds a sample to the grid. The sample is then available for students as a reminder of possible literature responses they can work on during center time.

Literacy Response Chart

WOW Wow Sheet	Character Frame
Create a Caption	Write an Ending
Label It	Make a Connection

Keeping Text Experiences at the Center of All Learning

Students must have time to interact with text in a variety of settings and for a variety of purposes. Books and print must be an integral part of every literacy center in your classroom. The more opportunities students have to reread and revisit familiar texts, the greater impact they will have on their comprehension and fluency.

Here are some suggestions for adding text to classroom centers:

- **Calendar:** Add the weather report from the newspaper for students to read.
- **Specials Schedule:** Near your specials list (i.e., art, music, P.E.), add appropriate books and articles about topics related to the specials. For example, if students have P.E., you could add a sports story; if they are going to music, you could post the latest review of a show or concert in your area.
- **Karaoke:** Susan's students love their new karaoke center where they practice reading familiar songs in preparation for Friday performances. When each student learns his or her selected song and demonstrates understanding of the words and vocabulary, then he or she can perform it for the class on Friday.
- **Word Work:** Keep a basket of simple alphabet books in this center.
- **Writing Center:** Add cartoons to your writing center for students to study dialogue.
- **Math Center:** Add toy catalogs and coupons for students to read and "shop" with.
- **Library:** Keep your book order forms in the Classroom Library. Students can look to see which books you have and which books they might like to add to the library.

From Mellissa: Sticky notes are great tools to add to all of your literacy centers. The sticky note can serve as a marker for specific places students want to remember in text. It also is a place where students can record their thoughts about their reading or writing. In my research center, I often have my students fill out the Properties Observation sheet on page 121 of this book. If they are looking at leaves, I try to add books about leaves to the center. Students use the sticky note to mark an interesting place in the text and add one or two facts from their observations to the note. The sticky notes can stay in the book for the next student to read or be added to our "Did You Know?" chart at this center.

Build an Extensive Classroom Library

If you do no other centers from this book, we suggest you do this one. If you want to build a classroom that helps students increase their reading and writing skills and transition them from emergent to fluent reading, then you must start with the Classroom Library. It is the heartbeat of your classroom. If we want our students to "read like writers and write like readers," then we must immerse them in meaningful print. They will never learn to read and write better until they have books and print in their hands on a regular basis.

A well-stocked Classroom Library can be utilized as a stand-alone center and fuel many other centers in your classroom. The more books students have access to, the better readers and writers they will become. We believe that ten books per student is a minimum-sized Classroom Library. Many teachers seek out grant funding, parent donations, and book clubs to provide materials for the Classroom Library.

Utilize student input as you organize the Classroom Library. Find out their favorite authors, what topics they are interested in, or which genres they enjoy. Then label your baskets and bins accordingly. This will make it easy for your students to find books quickly and return them to their proper place. Another way to begin organizing your library will require you to empty your bookshelves and start from scratch! At first this can seem like an overwhelming task, but the results are worth the investment of time. After you clear your shelves of all books, organize your collection of the books you already have. Do you have autographed or special titles you want to keep in a reserved section? Do you have several titles by a particular author? Do you have a collection of alphabet books? This is where you begin. Once these books have been organized into baskets, look for gaps in your collection. What

do you need to make your library complete? Use your book club points to help you fill the gaps and build a strong collection that encourages your readers to keep coming back for more.

Think about the appeal of bookstore cafés. What is it that makes people want to linger over a good book? Many of the books are easy to locate as they are displayed with the covers facing out. This grabs the reader's attention and invites book browsing. Think about which shelves are at eye-level for your students. Put the books that almost everybody can read on these shelves. Books that are more challenging should be placed in higher shelves while easier books can be stored on bottom shelves. Additionally, make sure that there are comfortable places to sit (or recline) and read. An effective Classroom Library is cozy and inviting to readers of all abilities. Make sure that all students can select and "read" the books that interest them. While there are times that you want kids to have a just-right book that they can read during independent reading, there are other times that they need to be encouraged to browse the challenging books even if they can't read the entire text. Young readers often pick up visual information from captions, labels, photos, or illustrations in these books. An effective Classroom Library will have a variety of titles, levels, and interests to satisfy the reading appetites in your class.

Remember to look back at interest inventories and student conference notes to address the needs of your students through your Classroom Library.

How can your Classroom Library support other centers in your room? Once students are comfortable with the selection of books in the classroom, these baskets can be moved to other locations around the room. A basket of informational texts can be placed in the Research Center for locating and reporting information. The magazine collection can be added to the Writing Center for students to use as models when writing an article about a current event. The poetry basket can be accessed in the Poetry Center to encourage rereading of favorite poems. A basket of books by a particular author

can be showcased in the Word Work center to record favorite words from that author's books. A collection of alphabet books is a great addition to the word wall for students to use when exploring how word-wall words can be found in many kinds of writing.

Is your Classroom Library the "hub" of literacy learning in your room? Use the following assessment checklist to determine the effectiveness of your current Classroom Library.

Classroom Library Assessment Checklist		
Question	Yes	No
1. Do I have at least ten quality children's literature books per child in my classroom?		
2. Are my books organized into baskets or tubs (by author, topic, and/or genre)?		
3. Do some books face out so that children can view the covers?		
4. Do the books cover a range of levels to meet the needs of all my students?		
5. Do all children have access to all of the books regardless of level?		
6. Can my books be checked out to take home or placed in independent reading baskets?		
7. Does my organizational system allow students to locate books on the shelves and properly return them after use?		
8. Are there comfortable places for children to read?		
9. Are students able to make suggestions and requests for adding new titles?		
10. Do I use books from my Classroom Library for other center opportunities?		

Chapter Four
I—Interacting as a Learning Community

"What is the use of a book," thought Alice, "without pictures or conversations?"

Lewis Carroll, *Alice's Adventures in Wonderland*

If you want kids to interact as a learning community, then you must model community during whole-class lessons, group and teach them well, set them up for success, make sure their environment is rich with learning opportunities, and make them responsible for what happens there. The very definition of community suggests that there is interdependence and interaction among members.

Students rehearse poems together to build fluency.

Whole-Class Lessons and Discussions

Literacy development is a social process. Students must have time to meaningfully interact with other adults and their peers if they are to properly acquire literacy skills and strategies. Think about it: If we want students to be better speakers, then we have to give them many opportunities to speak. If we want them to be able to listen to information, then we need to speak with them and give them those opportunities to listen to a wide range of speakers and auditory material.

From Susan: While working with my struggling second- and third-grade readers on asking questions before, during, and after reading, we created a list of questions that we had about a space book. Before reading, I wrote questions on a large chart as the children generated them. After reading, we revisited the chart we created and noted which questions were answered during our reading. The students were quick to notice that many of our questions remained unanswered. I asked, "How could we find answers to our questions?" and students gave suggestions. Corey said, "You could look in the dictionary." We had a brief discussion about what kinds of information we might find in the dictionary. Then I asked, "Where else could you look?" Ashley confidently stated, "You could look in the onomatopoeia." I hesitated for a moment as I thought. Then she said, "You know, you go there and look up something and it has articles about it." What she meant to say was, "You could look in the encyclopedia."

As I reflected on this unplanned lesson about reference materials, I realized how vital these conversations are for students. If Ashley didn't feel comfortable enough in our classroom to take a risk and speak up, I might never have known about the word confusion she had regarding reference materials. Oddly enough, when we look at the data from our state exam, the knowledge and understanding of reference materials is one of our weaker areas. Perhaps these conversations and our subsequent placement of multiple references in our Research Centers will help students understand a variety of reference materials and their purpose.

Our whole-class instruction should occasionally mirror the dinner table conversation. It should be a natural give and take of thoughts and ideas. Setting up this type of interaction takes time and training, however, because many students come to us with the notion that the teacher speaks and then one child responds. There is little, if any, conversation that happens from student to student during whole-class instruction.

To help students know when this type of conversation is welcomed and expected, you might want to create a class meeting place. Some teachers use a large rug, others use benches, and still others have students pull their individual desks into a large circle. Some teachers place a lamp in this special place. Students know that when the lamp is on, the give and take of conversation is expected and encouraged. Whatever you choose, make sure students know that it is OK to talk to one another *and* to you during this time. As you develop a community of learners in the classroom, this open conversation will become the norm and not the exception.

Grouping and Teaching

Before you group students for learning centers or any other small-group experience, you must know them well. Interview them. Find out what excites them and makes them tick. Use the "Student Interview" form on page 182 in the Teacher Resources to record a quick inventory of student likes and dislikes. Second-grade teacher Penny Varnum honors every child as a learner in her classroom. After finding out their interests, she begins looking for materials that will enhance their classroom experiences. She occasionally brings in an article or book that she found and announces to a specific child, "I found this and I knew you'd like to read it." Students immediately feel like their teacher knows them well.

Grouping is critical to center success. If a group is not able to work well together, consider making a change. Make sure that your groups are heterogenous and multi-level.

If a grouping that you make is not working, you might want to ask these questions:

- Do I have students in this group that are too much alike?
- What is the learning style of each person in this group?
- Does one child dominate the group?
- How can I work with this group to ensure center success?
- Would the change of one or two students make a difference?

From Susan: In my classroom, Briana really likes to talk. She seems to work out most of her problems orally. I know this and allow her to do it within predefined boundaries. I also know that Michael does not like to talk. He likes to focus quietly on the task he is given and work it out in his head. These individual styles work for each learner. When they were together in a group, however, they drove each other crazy. Briana would talk to Michael and he would get frustrated because she was interrupting his learning process. I had to match each of these learners with other students who would understand and respect their learning styles.

We encourage you to make your grouping a dynamic and ongoing process. Sometimes it takes a while to find the right mix of students. Ask your students what they think would work best when grouping. Remind them that "in this classroom, we can learn from everyone."

Occasionally, you will get a student who simply cannot or does not work well with others. You have to make some decisions at that point. Rather than shutting down centers altogether, we suggest using other methods. Susan has used a hula hoop near her guided reading table as a spot where the child could bring his or her materials and work there alone. Mellissa has used proximity where the child could work at a desk or table close to her. This allows her to redirect the student when necessary. There are many great books available on classroom management and discipline. If this is an area in which you struggle, we suggest that you research further ideas in any of these resources.

Forming groups of students is a proactive process where the teacher knows his or her students well enough to make decisions for their success, anticipate problems, and plan for a variety of strengths and areas of growth. It is also an experience based on trial and error. The intentional and responsive teacher will make adjustments as needed.

Teach Them Well

Most of us would agree that when we are given a new task to complete, we need to know the "why." Our students are no different. If we put something into a center for students to use, they need to know why it is important. If we put something in a center they do not know how to access, we have to back up and try again. Quality of experiences is more important than quantity. When we do this, then literacy center practice is a rich experience that truly helps them improve their skills and strategies.

> *From Mellissa:* *At my research center, I placed a set of magazines for students to begin a study on animals. I created a set of questions they could use for inquiry, and we also charted their questions to use for research. I thought I had modeled how to read articles enough in shared reading and guided reading to support this activity in centers. We also had a wide range of magazine selections in our Classroom Library. When I began to look at the research taking place, however, I noticed that many of my students struggled with this experience. I had a difficult time putting my finger on the source of the problem. I decided to conference with a couple of readers to see if they could help me discover the source of difficulty. After speaking with the children, we realized immediately what happened. Yes, the students were familiar with magazines, article structures, and features of informational text. What I had not shared with them is how magazines are structurally different from a single article. For example, the content of* Zoobooks *is dedicated to the one specific animal shown on the cover. The content of a* Ranger Rick *magazine includes articles on a variety of animals. I had not modeled this subtle difference because I had not seen its importance before that moment. Once the students and I understood this variable, the quality of process and product improved because now students were able to access the information they needed.*

Set Them up for Success

There are many things that you can do to set your students up for success in the classroom. We have to find ways to make them the stars of the thinking and learning. Some words we have heard teachers say that illustrates this message are in the following chart. Add some of your own phrases for a quick reference. Make these messages a regular part of your classroom talk.

I want you to be a great talker today…	That's really great thinking…
I want you to be a great listener today…	I share your thinking…
You really know how to use your brain…	Thank you for your contribution…
That's so smart…	Thank you for adding that to our thinking…

Success vs. Over-Support

Sometimes we have to support our learners as they work through rigorous texts and materials. The concept of scaffolding experiences is to temporarily support the learners as they try to extend their skills to a higher level. Scaffolding is not meant to make the task easier. The difficulty of the task remains the same while the teacher adjusts support in response to the learner's success. Over-support can lead to overdependence on the part of the learner. An example of scaffolding is strategy talk used in guided reading. As students come to points of difficulty in texts and are not sure of the comprehension strategies to use, the teacher gently prompts the reader to think about what they could try to do. Some readers will need a mini-lesson on how to employ a strategy while others will begin to self-monitor more regularly. This prompting later acts as a voice that tells the reader what they should be thinking about as they read. If the teacher prompts the reader on every miscue, the learner does not take control of the reading. The scaffold now becomes "over-support."

From Susan: One center area in which students might need some scaffolding at the beginning of the year is the Literature Response Center. I first model a variety of ways students can respond to books. We then create letters, summaries, connections, etc. I provide guided practice and collect response notebooks. Later, I confer with readers and help shape their responses as needed. Some of my students need an extra support in the form of a response scaffold. I only provide these when I see students really want to respond but are having difficulty organizing their thoughts. Once students feel more comfortable, I take that scaffold away so they can grow independently in their responses. (See the "Reader's Response" charts for both fiction and informational texts on the last two pages of this chapter.)

From Mellissa: When I am working with small groups I try to keep interruptions to a minimum. However, students need support at all times. Each day I select a center captain to field questions and concerns from group members. Center captains can go to other center captains in the room for support. If they cannot solve the problem, then a center captain may come to me for help. This minimizes the number of students interrupting my instruction, yet they can also get the help they need.

Keep the Environment Rich with Literacy Mentors

Open up your classroom doors to the world outside. Students need models of literacy mentors in their lives. These mentors can take the shape of other employees in your school, active community members, business partners, guest readers, students' family members, etc. Ask these guests to come in and share how literacy impacts their lives at home and on the job. Dedicate an area of the room where photos of visitors are displayed, and have students write about visitors' jobs at the Writing Center. Add books from the Media Center to support the new experiences children are learning about.

Reader's Response: Fiction

My Name: _____ Date:_____

The title of this book is

_____

The author of the book is

_____

My favorite part was when

_____
_____
_____

I liked this part because

_____
_____
_____

A connection I made to this book is

_____
_____
_____

Questions I have for the author are

1._____?
2._____?
3._____?

Reader's Response: Informational Text

My Name: _____ Date:_____

The title of this text is

_____

The author is

_____

I picked this text because

_____

The most important information is

_____

_____

_____

Three interesting facts I learned are

1. _____
2. _____
3. _____

After I read, I am still wondering...

1. _____
2. _____
3. _____

Words that were tricky in the text were

_____

_____

_____

Chapter Five
C—Conversations about Content

For many children, non-fiction opens the door to seeing a purpose for reading. As they use non-fiction resources to pursue their personal interests and hobbies, books and reading become an integral part of their lives, both in and out of the classroom.

Brenda Parkes, *Read It Again! Revisiting Shared Reading* (81)

As we present on literacy centers around the country, countless teachers tell us that they don't have "time to teach." When we delve a bit deeper, we usually find out that they have sacrificed explicit teaching of science and social studies to focus on reading, writing, and mathematics. Certainly it is true that no child can do science or social studies if he cannot read and write, but we don't believe that the instruction of these subjects should be excluded from the primary classroom either. Students deserve the opportunity to explore their world through hands-on activities, to develop and investigate questions about topics of interest, and to engage in critical conversations which promote active thinking and learning. Literacy centers can provide a venue in your classroom to enhance a naturally present trait in all children: curiosity.

Curriculum Mapping: Process and Product

As stated in Chapter 2, it is up to each individual teacher to be keenly aware of the curriculum expectations for his or her state and/or district. If "getting it all in" is an issue for you, then we suggest you spend some time either individually or with your colleagues looking at how to map out your curriculum.

You need to start by considering what you do currently. We find that many teachers are teaching the things they *love* without regard to the things they *need*. An example of this is the infamous dinosaur unit. Just because you love teaching about dinosaurs does not mean that it should take up four to six weeks of your instruction without regard to what else should be taught. You must start by carefully considering the content area standards for the grade level that you teach. Be willing to modify or omit the topics that you currently teach only because you love them.

Susan met with each grade level at her school a few years ago and helped them figure out what the "big pictures" were in their curriculum expectations. This meant breaking down each standard and benchmark and looking for ways to integrate and overlap science with social studies and language arts, etc. It also meant taking a good, long look at some beloved units and agreeing that they needed to be replaced with content that was required.

The second-grade team, for example, had to teach immigration and national monuments in social studies and wheels and pulleys in science. This lead to the development of a year-long thematic unit focused on transportation and movement of people in the world. Once this theme was established, it was broken down into mini-units of instruction using the resources at the school. It was amazing to see how many teachers weren't aware of the resources available to them right there at the school site. After they found out about their school's resources, teachers planned explicit instruction and identified the expectations they would teach during each mini-unit.

Once the curriculum is mapped out, it is easier to see overlaps and to "get it all in." Teachers and students alike feel more comfortable moving through the year with a purpose in mind. Mapping the curriculum in this way allows for seamless integration of learning, ongoing assessment checks, and data-driven teaching. If you choose to create curriculum maps, it is critical to have professional conversations about the student needs at your school. It is most important to learn from the process, not just develop a product.

Mellissa's school embraced the idea of creating instructional timelines to assist teachers with the overwhelming task of integrating standards across reading, writing, math, science, social studies, and word study. Grade-level teams met during the summer to create an instructional map. Some of the essential questions developed by the grade-level teams involved in this process were:

- How will these timelines be used?
- How often will we assess our students?
- How will we use the data to guide our teaching?
- How can one assessment serve more than one purpose?
- How can we be flexible in using the timelines?
- How often will professional learning communities meet to discuss the effectiveness of the timelines?

Remember that content integration should not equal content fragmentation. Students act as the compass as you create the curriculum map! For more information on curriculum mapping, see the following resources:

Jacobs, Heidi Hayes. *Getting Results with Curriculum Mapping*. Alexandria, VA: Association for Supervision and Curriculum Development, 2004.

Jacobs, Heidi Hayes. *Mapping the Big Picture: Integrating Curriculum & Assessment K-12*. Alexandria, VA: Association for Supervision and Curriculum Development, 1997.

Tomlinson, Carol Ann. *The Differentiated Classroom: Responding to the Needs of All Learners*. Alexandria, VA: Association for Supervision and Curriculum Development, 1999.

Using Literary Texts to Teach Content Areas

Help students look for learning opportunities as you introduce literary text in your classroom. One interesting study Susan did with her first-graders centered around Cynthia Rylant's book, *The Relatives Came* (Atheneum, 1985). After reading this book, students began to discuss where their relatives live. Some lived right in town while others lived far away. As part of our social studies unit on using maps, students researched the location of their favorite relatives. Then they put a sticker on the map to identify geographical locations.

Writing Center Connection

In the Writing Center, students wrote what it was like visiting the place where their favorite relatives live. We informed students that it was OK to count someone next door or down the street if necessary. The maps and the text were placed in the Writing Center to invite students to revisit, reread, and reflect. The students practiced map-reading skills and improved writing skills and strategies as they completed this activity.

Research Center Connection

Look at your readers' workshop block. Where can you integrate content teaching into your literary program? During shared reading, Mellissa used the trade book series, *The Boxcar Children*, to launch a mystery genre study. In order to understand the coral reef setting of *The Mystery of the Hidden Beach* by Gertrude Chandler Warner (Albert Whitman & Company, 1994), Mellissa also read an informational text titled *Life in the Coral Reef* by Melvin Berger (Newbridge Educational Publishing, 1994). Comparing the informational text with the literary text provided the students with a rich context for building schema about coral reefs and for discovering how this information was critical in understanding the development of the plot. At the Research Center, Mellissa added a variety of books on coral reefs. Students posted inquiry questions on a chart displayed in the center. She also set up an aquarium with artifacts for students to touch and observe. Students recorded their observations and summarized their findings.

Many literary texts lend themselves to content-area teaching and learning. Make a list of some of your favorites and match them up with your standards and benchmarks. You just might be surprised at the goldmine that is sitting right inside your classroom!

Informational Texts and Literacy Centers

Literacy centers should engage student exploration in both literary and informational texts. Students need to be exposed to a wide variety of genre through the Classroom Library, whole- and small-group instruction, and independent literacy activities. We love our picture books and favorite authors and illustrators. Do we love our informational texts as well? Almost eighty percent of what an adult reads each day is informational. Think about it! Make a list of what you read today. It might look like ours.

- Bills
- Newspaper
- Magazine
- E-mail
- Road signs
- Food labels
- Medicine bottles
- Professional books

Now think about the amount of informational text you share with students daily. Today's teachers are fortunate to have a wide selection of informational texts for younger readers. Many publishers have added informational texts to their menu of options. However, not all informational books are of the highest quality. When selecting informational texts to use in your classroom, ask yourself the following questions:

- Does the collection have a range of levels to meet the needs of my students?
- Are the topics of interest to readers at this grade level?
- How are informational text features gradually introduced at various levels (photographs, captions, glossary, index, table of contents, graphs, charts, etc.)?
- Do texts allow for shared reading as well as guided reading?
- Do the teacher resource guides provide excellent models for high-level questioning and extension activities that encourage students to revisit the text to confirm and further their learning?

As you model strategies for reading across genres, it is important to place these texts within your centers to allow students to become comfortable with text features, structures, and content. Informational texts easily have a place at the Writing Center, Word Work Center, Listening Center, Research Center, Poetry, Classroom Library, and Literature Response Center. Reading is an active "hands-on, minds-on" process. Books should freely pass from your hands to theirs; students should buzz about new ideas and learning; and conversations should be encouraged throughout the classroom. Who knows? You could have a future inventor sitting in your classroom right now!

Content-Area Instruction and the Struggling Reader

Matching students to texts using book levels is just one way to support the struggling reader. One of the most powerful motivators for young, struggling readers is to find out what interests they have and then use them to encourage reading and writing. Students come to your class with a wide range of experiences and preferences. When teachers tap into the lives of students and bring their interests into the classroom, learning becomes powerful. Students see a connection between their world and school. Children are honored and celebrated.

For example, Mellissa worked with struggling readers in a small-group setting. While with the group, she liked to find out what interests each student had, such as dirt-biking, dance, drama, football, etc. She asked each student to share what he or she knew about their interest area. This lead to rich discussions as students became classroom experts in these areas of interest. She recorded the information on a chart for students to use as a reference. Anyone who needed to know something about dinosaurs went to Andrew. Others knew to talk to Justice if they wanted to learn about sports.

The "Be the Expert" literacy center (see page 150) was developed from this experience. Not only did the valuable information on students' interests assist Mellissa in choosing books with children, it also created a community of learners and teachers in the classroom. The students knew that the teacher was not the only expert in the class.

Grades and Literacy Centers

Over and over again we are asked about how to get grades for science and social studies. Many teachers use literacy center projects for grades in these content areas. We would like to caution you about assuming that, because a child completes a center activity, he or she has mastered a particular content area standard. For example, if he or she creates a diorama on the Amazon Rainforest after reading a book about rainforests, it does not indicate that he or she understands ecosystems.

Make sure your centers are aligned with your curriculum standards. Remember that at least eighty percent of what kids do in centers is practice reading and writing, which should *not* be graded. Centers can allow for meaningful practice, but it is the process that matters, not just a final product. While we do *not* recommend that centers be used for grading, we do encourage teachers to use this opportunity for assessment. By collecting some products, observing students, and taking anecdotal records, as well as conferencing with readers, you will reflect on the quality of your centers and make adjustments to your instruction.

Chapter Six
K—Keeping the Focus

As professionals, we are the most important condition in the room. It is our literacy and the quality of inquiry in our own lives that provide the tone and the quality of learning in the children's lives. So much of learning is picked up while observing another person learn and do things. The children observe us each day from September through June in the ways in which we solve human problems between and among children. They witness our demonstrations and our lines of inquiry in our reading, writing, and solutions to mathematical problems.

Donald H. Graves, *The Energy To Teach* (45)

Many things cloud our focus in the primary classroom. There are lesson plans to write, state mandates to follow, district maps to implement, and assessments to administer. But the reality is none of these things matter if we don't think about the students we teach and their individual needs and abilities. Our students need to be at the core of every decision made regarding lesson planning and implementation. Let's explore ways to keep the focus when implementing and practicing literacy centers in the classroom.

Know What You Do and Why You Do It

We can both recall many years of teaching where we simply turned the page and followed the next lesson down an imaginary learning path. Most textbook publishers will say that they develop lessons with the student in mind. However, these publishers don't know the specific students who walk in and out your door each and every day. You do. More and more publishers seem to be giving teachers a menu of ideas to differentiate the instruction in their classrooms. Therefore, it is more critical and more possible than ever to make informed instructional decisions.

Teaching and learning are dynamic. They change from year to year based on the students in your class, their own cultural and social backgrounds, your professional beliefs, and the district or state curriculum. Once you make informed decisions regarding what is best for your students instructionally, you need to be able to articulate what you do and why you do it.

Traditionally, it has been assumed that knowledge alone is the key to improved teaching. But research on effective teaching indicates that the best teachers take charge of professional knowledge, manipulate it, and adapt it to changing instructional situations. We find the most successful teachers are those who stand firm in their own pedagogy and are also open to new ideas and current research. For us, reading professional resources, attending professional conferences, and collaborating with colleagues about what works for them helps us make informed decisions about our classroom practices.

As with teaching in general, literacy center practice must be purposeful and revolve around on student learning. It is so much more than keeping kids busy so you can teach small groups. Nor is it a glorified worksheet. Practice and application of skills and strategies in literacy centers have the potential to move students further down their literacy path. When they engage in reading and writing text in centers and when the conditions are right for learning, students are likely to acquire new skills and strategies.

If we want our classrooms to be rich places of learning, then it's important for us to be self-reflective. We need to think about what has worked and what changes (if any) need to be made. Use the following reflections to help guide your thinking further about what you do and why you do it.

Reflection One: If you are new to centers
- Why do you want to start using centers?
- What excites you about using centers in your classroom?
- What concerns you?
- How will you make your centers relevant to your students and their learning needs?
- How will you make your centers multi-level?

Reflection Two: If you already use centers
- Which centers worked really well for you and your students?
- Which centers might you need to abandon or rework?
- How can you increase the quality of your centers?
- Do your centers take students deeper into understanding?
- How can you evoke further conversation in your literacy centers?

Refocus and Adjust when Necessary

Have you ever looked through a pair of binoculars? The object has come into view: crisp, vivid, and clear. Suddenly, you shift your gaze for a moment and everything becomes blurry. With a quick click of the dial, the object becomes clear again and all is well. Literacy centers, too, can have moments of cloudiness. Should you change your centers? Should you make the centers more challenging? Should you just give up on centers this year? Occasionally, keeping the focus is hard. It means that you have to be willing to make necessary changes to keep your literacy center time effective for students. Each classroom is a unique place of learning and requires your expertise when making the right decisions for your students. The following challenges are common when implementing centers in a classroom. We have provided a few suggestions that have worked for us. Remember to engage in productive conversations with your colleagues, read professional resources, and self-reflect as you make ongoing decisions about your learning community this year.

Solutions to Common Problems in the Centers

How should I group students in centers?

Students should be grouped heterogeneously in centers. If you send five to seven students to two center areas in your classroom, then call out two for guided reading, you have reduced the number of students working independently in the center. Grouping should be flexible and dynamic. If a group of students is not working, change it. Sometimes it takes several changes to group effectively.

What should I do when a center just doesn't work?

Sometimes a center is not effective with a group of students. If this happens, think back to the conditions for learning: immersion, demonstration, expectation, responsibility, approximations, employment (use), and response. Ask yourself what adjustments can be made to the center in order to maximize learning. Have you modeled what is expected, provided time for students to practice, and monitored with feedback as needed? Maybe you just need to clean the lens and refocus instead of giving up on a center. Think about what you want students to gain from participating in a particular center, and ask yourself if you have provided them enough support to meet the goal.

What should I do when kids mistreat the materials?

Teachers often put new tools and materials into centers without proper introduction. If students are mistreating things, it is time to have a class meeting. Call everyone together and talk about the problem. Be specific about the problem and invite students to brainstorm solutions. Ask students to help you identify appropriate ways to behave in centers. Record student responses on a chart and display it at the center. Model these expected behaviors as well as how not to act at the centers.

How can I prevent the students from rushing through the center and producing low-quality work?

We have all experienced frustration with "I'm done" syndrome. Look carefully at the activities and materials you have provided in the center. Is it the same student who is always finished in a hurry? If so, have an individual conference with that student to explain why you feel he or she can do better quality work. Are many students finishing quickly? Perhaps there are not enough opportunities for different levels of students in the center. Adding books to all centers increases time in text as well as provides students meaningful reading practice. If they complete a task at a center, they can always curl up with a good book and enjoy. Remember: You are never done reading. When you finish reading one book, start another!

Sometimes students simply need help managing their time at centers. We attended a training by Linda Holliman and adapted a four-pocket center folder idea for management. Susan also tried out the system and described its use in *So Much Stuff, So Little Space: Creating and Managing the Learner-Centered Classroom* (Maupin House, 2002). Our goal in implementing this strategy was to help students reflect on the quality of their work. Not all centers required a finished product, but this folder allowed students to keep track of their learning while serving as a quick assessment tool for the teacher .

Outside of work folder:

You've Got Mail	(Student's Name) **To be done**

Inside of work folder:

Working	Finished

Mellissa had students place any products from centers in a four-pocket folder. Pockets were labeled with four headings:

- **Student Name:** This pocket was located on the front of the folder and held the center contract students completed as they worked through centers. Mellissa checked the contract with the student work found inside the folder. She used it as a conferencing tool with students.
- **Working:** This left-side pocket was located inside the folder. Students kept their ongoing work in the pocket. Mellissa knew that not all activities could be completed in one day's time. Many experiences were ongoing, and this pocket gave students a way to organize those activities without feeling penalized.
- **Finished:** This right-side pocket was located inside the folder. Students placed their completed activities in this pocket when they were ready for Mellissa to give feedback. She checked these pieces against the contract and again conferenced with readers.
- **You've Got Mail:** This pocket was located on the back of the folder. Mellissa laminated little red "mailbox" flags and attached one to each pocket with a bracket. When she wanted to give students feedback, she placed a note in the pocket and raised the flag. She would place notes about behavior, quality of work, and observations about how the student was growing as a reader. The notes were positive motivators for students, who looked forward to checking their mailboxes.

How do I encourage a group to get along and not tattle on each other during center time?

Community, community, community! In *Reading with Meaning: Teaching Comprehension in the Primary Grades* (Stenhouse, 2002), Debbie Miller states, "Real classroom communities are more than just a look. Real communities flourish when we bring together the voices, hearts, and souls of the people who inhabit them."

Think back to the first days of school. How will you establish community this year? You can have mini-lessons on how to get along. You can provide students with a list of possible sentence-starters to help take the edge off of their complaints. You can redirect student behavior that has gone astray. However, you are the key to this community. What do you really want for your students this year? Is it to complete all of their center work in a timely manner with a wide, toothless grin? Or perhaps you really want them to learn and grow not only from your teaching but from each other. This learning means being responsive to children's likes, dislikes, similarities, differences, interests, strengths, and needs. It also means helping children become tolerant and civil.

How students talk with each other is a big indicator of the classroom community established by the teacher. Conversations should flow easily and not be controlled by the teacher as interrogator. Students must learn how to respond to the different personalities in the room. At the beginning of the year during readers' workshop, Mellissa models how students can "piggyback" their responses off each other. She models how to listen to another student and add to the discussion. Sometimes she agrees, questions, or disagrees with a reader. But her responses are always given with respect, courtesy, and civility. Together they create a list of options students can try when conversing with each other. Depending on the age of the group, the list might look like this:

- I agree because…
- I disagree because…
- I'd like to add that…
- That reminds me of…
- That's a good point because…
- Can you explain what you mean by…
- I was thinking something different when…

Julie Sparks, a third-grade teacher, uses a community message board in her classroom for students to share questions, concerns, needs, or suggestions. Students place their comments on sticky notes and display them on the message board during center time. This allows students to get their thinking down without interrupting her small group instruction. She reads the messages daily and conferences with the learners on an as needed basis. Here are some student messages from Julie's class:

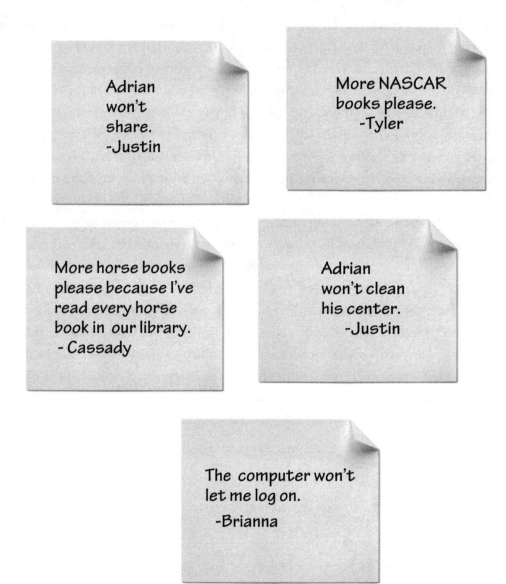

Julie reflected on the community messages and realized the following:

- She could make some adjustments to the Classroom Library.
- She needed to conference with Adrian and Justin.
- She could have another student help Brianna with the computer.

Susan's son, Aaron, began kindergarten this year. His teacher, Judi Blessee, has established a powerful classroom community that is now spreading to Susan's home. After a disagreement with his older brothers, Aaron announced to the family, "You are not following the three-step rule!" Judi's three-step rule was continuously modeled throughout the year, and it had a huge impact on Aaron's problem-solving behaviors:

1. You name what happened.
2. Tell how it made you feel.
3. You ask them to stop and do something different.

Establishing a caring and collaborative environment creates a setting for learning that reaches far beyond the classroom walls. The impact of this community is seen and felt not when you are standing in front of the classroom telling children how to behave but in the quiet corners and busy tables when you are a silent witness to the magic of children sharing learning with each other.

How do I really know what my students are gaining from centers?

Susan has students write their reflections on the day's learning on an "exit card." This index card is the student's ticket to exit from her class. Students can write about what they did that day to help them become a better reader and writer; they can write about suggestions for centers, books they want, and ways Susan can facilitate their learning; they can write about *anything* they want! These powerful two- to three-line reflections give Susan important information about her students' thinking, perceptions, and learning journey. More importantly, it sends a message to her students—she cares about them and is willing to make adjustments to her teaching from their input.

One student's exit card requested more Margie Palatini books in the classroom. This student was normally quiet and never would have made this request in front of others. Susan conferenced with the reader, pulled out a book club order form, and created a wish list with the student. She used her book club bonus points and ordered these books for the classroom. The exit card provided a safe haven for the child, honored a realistic request, and involved the learner in the process. Quickly, this idea caught on and other students began requesting books. As not every request could be met with a book order, students were encouraged to learn about the valuable resources available in the school's media center.

Part Two
Literacy Connectiom
Planners

Chapter Seven
Reading Connections

> 1. **Strategies for Learning and Using Words:** Readers use their understanding of word identification and meaning during text interaction.
>
> 2. **Strategies for Comprehension:** Readers construct meaning from a variety of text.
>
> 3. **Strategies for Finding Information:** Readers gather, evaluate, and synthesize data and information from a variety of sources.
>
> 4. **Strategies for Building Fluency and Independence:** Readers self-select appropriate text and read for a variety of purposes.

1. Strategies for Learning and Using Words: Readers use their understanding of word identification and meaning during text interaction.

Page	Mini-Lesson Topic	Literacy Center Connection	Center Title
52	Using sound/symbol relationships to segment and blend words	Word Work	"Copy Me"
54	Connecting the known to the new	Listening	"Word Builders"
56	Monitoring comprehension by highlighting text	Word Work	"Highlight It"
60	Strategies for learning and using words	Word Work	"Magic Words"

Mini-Lesson: Using sound/symbol relationships to segment and blend words

Materials: Magnetic letters, word cards with high-frequency words, pencil
Reader's and Writer's Workshop Component: Word Work

1. Explain to your students that they will be helping you make words using magnetic letters.

2. Choose several high-frequency words from a shared reading or read-aloud book the children have heard several times.

3. Hold up an index card and say the first word. Ask, "Who can name the first letter in this word?" When a student identifies the letter, let her come up and find its match from the magnetic letters. Then ask, "Who knows the next letter in this word?" Continue in this fashion until the word has been spelled out with the magnetic letters.

4. Help students read the word slow so they can hear the segmented sounds while you run your hand under the letters. Then read it fast so they can think about how it would sound in context.

5. Continue in this manner until you have made several words with the magnetic letters.

6. Review the list with your students.

7. Encourage one or two children to try and write one or two words on the board.

Mini-Lesson Notes

Literacy Center Connection: Word Work

Center Title: "Copy Me"

Place the magnetic letters in your Word Work center. Place several index cards with the words printed on them. Encourage students to copy and spell the words using the magnetic letters.

After they copy, they may choose one or two words to practice writing on the whiteboards or on paper. Remind students that when they are through, all letters must be put away properly.

Lesson Variations and Notes

- Store magnetic letters in large cookie tins. Children will enjoy making words on the lids.
- Periodically add new word cards that correspond with your shared-reading mini-lessons.
- Encourage students to find similarities and differences in the words they copy.
- With the youngest learners, have them begin by copying their friends' names.
- Include spelling lists, word lists using phonograms or word patterns, or vocabulary lists in this center.

From Mellissa: In my first-grade classroom, my students and I would occasionally select one or two words from our word wall to be used in this center. This helped my students remember to use the word wall at other times during the day. Then they recorded the words on their personal word walls.

☐ Comprehension
☐ Fluency
☐ Phonemic Awareness
☑ Phonics
☑ Vocabulary

Mini-Lesson: Connecting the known to the new

Materials: Cassette player, cassette tapes with teacher-recorded directions, magnetic letters,
cookie sheets (magnetic surface)

Reader's Workshop Component: Shared Reading

1. Reread a familiar text from a Big Book, chart, or overhead.
2. Select a word from the text that would serve as an anchor for building other words.
3. Begin with a think-aloud: "Sometimes when I am reading I come to a word I do not know. It helps for me to think of another word like it. I look for patterns in the word to help me. For example, I noticed the -ook pattern in this word in another story I was reading. It reminds me of the word "book," but this word starts with the letter "c." This word must be "cook" then.
4. Have students help you create a list of words following the "ook" pattern. Model by using magnetic letters on the overhead and record the words on a chart.
5. Provide practice with another word such as "like." Have students work in pairs to make a list of other words that follow the "-ike" pattern. Explain how anchor words help you read and write new words.

Mini-Lesson Notes

Literacy Center Connection: Listening

Center Title: "Word Builders"

Supply this center with a cassette player (headphones optional), audio-taped directions, magnetic letters, and a magnetic surface (cookie sheets work well). Review student reading records and writing samples to determine the focus for student practice in this center. Record a set of systematic word-building directions for students to listen to as they build words using the magnetic letters. Keep these directions simple and easy to manage as you introduce this center. Gradually increase the level of difficulty based on your students' needs. See "Lesson Variations and Notes" below for some suggestions.

Lesson Variations and Notes

- Use commercial reading and writing program materials to find lesson ideas.
- Ask your media specialist for a resource to order ten-minute cassettes. Label and file cassettes by phonetic elements (word families, spelling patterns, vowel combinations, etc.).
- Have older readers use a clipboard and paper to record words they have built. Use this information as an assessment opportunity.
- Storage Tip: Use a fishing tackle box or a craft box with several small drawers to store and organize magnetic letters.
- For ideas on systematic word-building activities see *Making Words* by Patricia M. Cunningham and Dorothy P. Hall (Good Apple, 1994).

☐ Comprehension
☐ Fluency
☑ Phonemic Awareness
☑ Phonics
☑ Vocabulary

Mini-Lesson: Monitoring comprehension by highlighting text

Materials: Transparency and copies of an article, newsletter, or poem; highlighters; "Highlight It!" sheet (page 58); "Word Solvers" sheet (page 59)

Reader's Workshop Component: Shared Reading

1. Model strategies for self-monitoring with a new text.

2. Display a copy of the text on an overhead transparency.

3. Begin with a think-aloud: "Sometimes when I am reading I come to a word I do not know how to pronounce. Follow along as I read this sentence. (Read a sentence from the text that has a difficult word in it.)

4. As you read, stop and highlight a word that might be tricky to say. Continue to think aloud: "There are strategies I could use to help me figure out how to say this word. I could chunk it. I could skip it and read to the end of the sentence to find clue words to help me. Maybe I could think of another word that looks like this word. Which strategy do you think would really help me with this word?"

5. Ask students for input and decide together on the best strategy for the word you are problem-solving.

6. Create a class chart titled "Word Solvers," and record different strategies for solving unknown words. Use the sheet on page 59 as a reference. Display the chart at the Word Work Center.

7. As a follow up to this lesson, model the concept of highlighting words students can pronounce but do not understand. Create a class chart titled "What Does It Mean?" Record strategies to help students monitor for meaning. (Page 59 has some strategy suggestions that you may want to reference as you create the charts above with your students.)

Mini-Lesson Notes

Literacy Center Connection: Word Work

Center Title: "Highlight It!"

Make copies of a magazine article, classroom newsletter, poem, etc. Provide students with a highlighter and the "Highlight It!" sheet (page 58). Have students read through the selection and highlight words they cannot pronounce or understand. Encourage students to also highlight phrases they may find confusing. Students record the words or phrases they identify on the "Highlight It!" sheet. They can work with a buddy to use strategies they have learned during Reader's Workshop to solve unknown words.

Lesson Variations and Notes

- Give students removable highlighter tape to identify words in books. Highlighter tape can be placed on laminated index cards for easy removal and storage.

- Review the words or phrases students have identified as tricky. Use this information as an informal assessment to guide your readers' workshop lessons on word work and comprehension.

- Use multiple colors of highlighter tape to identify the different types of word-solving challenges. For example:
  - o Yellow = I can't say this word
  - o Orange = I don't know what this word means
  - o Pink = I don't understand this phrase

| ☑ Comprehension |
| ☐ Fluency |
| ☐ Phonemic Awareness |
| ☑ Phonics |
| ☑ Vocabulary |

Highlight It!

I can't say these words (in yellow):

I don't know what these words mean (in orange):

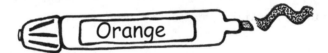

I don't understand these phrases (in pink):

Word Solvers

1.   Find tricky words.

2.   Chunk parts you know.

3.   Skip to the end of the sentence for clues and go back to   figure out what you don't know!)

4.   Think of words that look like the tricky word.

5.   Know where to find help.

What Does It Mean?

1.   Look for clues around the tricky word.

2.   Read on and come back.

3.   Get help from a friend, another book, charts around the room, or the dictionary.

4.   Use the glossary if the book has one.

Mini-Lesson: Sharing information with others to learn

Materials: Guided reading text, 4" x 6" index cards, school glue or hot glue, newsprint, crayons
Reader's Workshop Component: Guided Reading

1. Select several high-frequency words from a developmentally-appropriate guided reading book.

2. Use glue to write the words on an index card. (Note: to keep the words a bit more hidden, do not pre-write them on the card in pen/pencil.) Let the glue dry overnight. When the glue dries, the word will be tactile.

3. After you finish reading the book, say, "I have some magic words from our book. I am going to give you a magic word card, a crayon, and a piece of newspaper. Lay your piece of newsprint on top of your word card. Rub your crayon over the newsprint and find the magic word. When you can see the word clearly, put your crayon down." (Note: You may have to demonstrate crayon rubbing for some children.)

4. Students can practice reading their magic words and share them with the group.

5. Ask each student to locate his or her word in the guided reading book. Remind students that these are words that might appear more than once.

6. Have students see if they can locate their magic word somewhere else in the classroom (i.e., other books, classroom charts, word wall, etc.)

7. Trade cards and let each student find a new magic word.

Mini-Lesson Notes

Literacy Center Connection: Word Work

Center Title: "Magic Words"

Place several large 5" x 8" index cards with magic words on them in your Word Work Center. Make a "Magic Words" book for each student in your classroom. You can make this book by folding four to six pieces of newsprint in half and stapling them together. Students can use their books to find magic words doing crayon rubbings. When more advanced students figure out the magic words, have them use the words in a sentence.

Lesson Variations and Notes

- For more emergent readers, you may want to make letter cards. Students can practice finding words that start with their magic letter.
- If you want to focus on a single word from a book, give all students a word card with the same word on it.
- You may want to select only one word each week to focus on in your Word Work Center.

☐ Comprehension
☐ Fluency
☐ Phonemic Awareness
☑ Phonics
☑ Vocabulary

2. Strategies for Comprehension: Readers construct meaning from a variety of text.

Page	Mini-Lesson Topic	Literacy Center Connection	Center Title
63	Sequencing events from a story	Literature Response	"B, M, E: Beginning, Middle, End"
65	Reconstructing text for understanding	Classroom Library	"Reconstruct It!"
67	Activating prior knowledge	Classroom Library	"What Do I Know?"
71	Identifying the main character	Literature Response	"V.I.C.: Very Important Character"

Mini-Lesson: Sequencing events from a story

Materials: Precut letters "B," "M," and "E"; glue; read-aloud books; crayons or markers;
12" x 18" construction paper

Reader's Workshop Component: Read-Aloud

1. Choose a fiction read-aloud that has a clear beginning, middle, and end.

2. Before reading the book, say: "I know that fiction books often have a beginning, middle, and end. Let's think about a book we have read, like *Goldilocks and the Three Bears*. In the beginning, the bears decide to go for a walk so their porridge can cool. In the middle, Goldilocks breaks into the bears' house and tries their porridge, sits in their chairs, and falls asleep in their beds! In the end, the bears come home and find Goldilocks. Then she runs away and they never see her again. Today we are going to read a new book. I want you to listen and try to help me decide what happens in the beginning, middle, and end of the story."

3. Read the book to your class.

4. After you read the book, ask your students to help you identify what happens in each part of the story. Use a large piece of construction paper labeled "B" (for beginning), "M" (for middle), and "E" (for end) to record student responses.

5. Display this sample in your Literature Response Center.

Mini-Lesson Notes

Literacy Center Connection: Literature Response

Center Title: "B, M, E: Beginning, Middle, End"

Prior to beginning this center, cut out several lowercase "B," "M," and "E" letters using your die-cut machine or a pattern. Place the letters in a box labeled "B, M, E." When students are ready to respond to a book they have read, they can fold a sheet of paper into thirds and glue the "b" to the beginning, the "m" to the middle, and the "e" to the end. Then they can illustrate and write their retelling in the appropriate space. Display your students' "B, M, E" sheets in your literature response center for students to refer to when they read and write the room.

Lesson Variations and Notes

- To assess sequencing and comprehension, have your whole group complete a "B, M, E" sheet using the same book. Check to see that each child includes important details or pictures for each part of the story.

- Emergent readers and writers can illustrate what happened in the story.

- Volunteers can prepare the sheets for student use. Pre-fold the paper and glue the letters so the sheets are ready when students are ready to use them.

- Store all the materials required for a "B, M, E" sheet in a large manila envelope. Students can take it to their seats to use in their responses.

This student has selected a "B,M,E" from the Literacy Response Chart as a follow-up to the story he read.

From Susan: *After I cut the letters from the school's die-cut machine, I store them in a baby wipes container. I attach one set of the letters to the outside of the box as a label. This container is easily accessible to students during the Literature Response Center.*

☑ **Comprehension**
☐ **Fluency**
☐ **Phonemic Awareness**
☐ **Phonics**
☑ **Vocabulary**

Mini-Lesson: Reconstructing text for understanding

Materials: Guided reading text, sentence strips or tagboard, storage bags with plastic zippers
Reader's Workshop Component: Guided Reading

1. Pre-print sentences from a familiar guided reading text on small pieces of tagboard. For added durability, laminate the sentences.
2. Have students begin by rereading the familiar text.
3. Talk to students about understanding the book. Say, "When I read, sometimes I check to make sure I understand by telling someone else what is in my book. This is called retelling the story. Today we are going to practice retelling our story with a friend. I have some sentences from the story to help you remember it."
4. Give each student a sentence or two from the text. Guide the group to reconstruct the text in order using the book for support as needed.
5. Remind students that the way they figure out the order is by talking and thinking about the book they just read.
6. Let them practice in pairs with another book.

Mini-Lesson Notes

Literacy Center Connection: Classroom Library

Center Title: "Reconstruct It!"

Place copies of familiar shared- and guided-reading texts in your Classroom Library. Write the text of the book on small sentence strips or cut-up tagboard. Place these in a zippered storage bag. Students take the sentence strips and can use the book to reconstruct the text. When they finish, they can read the book or the sentence strips to a friend.

Lesson Variations and Notes

- Store sentence strips from individual books in gallon-sized, plastic bags with zippers. Insert a copy of the book. Store them in a box or basket labeled "Reconstruct It!"
- Bags with sentence strips can also be hung on a clothesline with clothespins under your board.
- Emergent readers can practice matching text directly to the book.
- Readers who are working with longer text can be given a portion of the book to reconstruct.

From Mellissa: When I work with kindergarten and first-grade students, I like to have them practice something called "pre-telling." During the morning class time, students work together to "pre-tell" what the procedures and routines will be in the classroom for that day. Sometimes we record these on a chart. This simple discussion where they sequence familiar procedures and routines helps students better understand the process of retelling text. This is also a great way to remind students what is expected of them during the literacy center block.

☑ **Comprehension**
☑ **Fluency**
☐ **Phonemic Awareness**
☐ **Phonics**
☑ **Vocabulary**

Mini-Lesson: Activating prior knowledge

Materials: Informational shared- or guided-reading text, "What Do I Know?" form from page 69 copied on a chart or overhead, directions for "What Do I Know?"

Reader's Workshop Component: Shared or Guided Reading

1. Print the "What Do I Know?" directions from page 70 on an overhead or chart paper.

2. Say, "When I pick up a new informational text, I have to think about what I already know about the topic. This helps me understand what I am reading. For example, if I pick up a book about frogs, I know that frogs hop, they grow from tadpoles, they lay eggs, and they eat insects. Thinking about these things helps me think about words that I might read in the book."

3. Display the new shared or guided reading text for students. Ask students to share what they know about the topic of the text with a partner.

4. After partners talk, let them share one or two things with the whole group. Record their answers on the "What Do I Know?" form or overhead transparency.

5. Explain that thinking about what you know helps you prepare your brain for reading. It signals your brain to begin thinking about the vocabulary you might read in the book.

6. After the reading, ask students to compare the words and information from the chart to the words and information found in the text. Discuss similarities and differences they find.

7. Let students practice in pairs with another book.

Mini-Lesson Notes

Literacy Center Connection: Classroom Library

Center Title: "What do I Know?"

Place a basket filled with informational books or articles in your Classroom Library. Make sure these are high-interest books at a variety of levels. Provide several copies of the "What Do I Know?" form from page 69 in this center along with the laminated directions. Students can select a book or an article and fill out the form.

Lesson Variations and Notes

- Laminate the "What Do I Know?" directions on page 70 to a closed file folder. Place blank copies of the "What Do I Know?" form inside the folder for easy access.
- This activity can be part of your Research Center.
- Emergent readers and writers can draw pictures on the "What Do I Know?" form instead of writing.

☑ Comprehension
☑ Fluency
☐ Phonemic Awareness
☐ Phonics
☑ Vocabulary

✔ What do I KNOW? ✔

1. Choose a book or article from the basket.

2. Think about the topic of the book or article.

3. Ask yourself, "What do I already KNOW about _____?"

4. Write some of the important things you know already on the form.

5. Read the book.

6. Write how thinking about what you KNOW about a topic helped you.

What do I KNOW?

Name: _____   Date: _____

Book Title: _____
Topic: _____

This is what I already KNOW:

How did this help me when I read the book?

Mini-Lesson: Identifying the main character

Materials: Chart paper, markers, familiar fiction book, "V.I.C.: Very Important Character" form
(page 73)

Reader's Workshop Component: Read-Aloud

1. Read aloud a familiar fiction text for enjoyment.

2. Discuss how identifying and knowing about the main character is important for understanding the events in a story. Begin with a think-aloud: "When I read a book with many characters, I understand the story better when I know who the most important character in the story is. That character is usually on most of the pages and talks with the other characters. The very important character usually has a problem to solve. Let's look back at the book we just read. I wonder how I could tell which character is most important."

3. Create a chart titled, "V.I.C.: Very Important Character."

4. Guide students' thinking about identifying the main character and record their responses on the chart. Responses might include observations about how the character talks the most, is on every page, has a problem, is in the title, etc.

5. Display the "V.I.C." chart and have students look through a different familiar text to identify the important character. Have them share with the group how they determined the "V.I.C." using the language from the class chart.

Mini-Lesson Notes

Literacy Center Connection: Literature Response

Center Title: "V.I.C.: Very Important Character"

Display the class-made "V.I.C." chart next to a basket of familiar fiction books. Have students select a book and complete the "V.I.C." form to identify the main character of the story. Students then highlight the statements about the "V.I.C." that pertain to their book. Students can share and compare their "V.I.C." forms with other students who read the same book.

Lesson Variations and Notes

- Refer to the "V.I.C." chart during guided reading. This will enable students to practice the strategy in texts they can read.

- Younger children may draw a picture of the "V.I.C."

- For more complex texts, modify the lesson to include strategies for identifying more than one main character. Staple several "V.I.C." forms together to create a book of the most important characters in a story.

- Use the "V.I.C." forms to make character connections. Ask students to identify how they are the same as or different from their selected characters.

- Have students make character connections to other people they know. Who does the "V.I.C." remind them of?

- Have students keep their "V.I.C." forms in a folder. When they have completed several charts, they can go back and compare and contrast characters from different stories.

☑ **Comprehension**
☑ **Fluency**
☐ **Phonemic Awareness**
☐ **Phonics**
☐ **Vocabulary**

V.I.C.

Book Title: _____.

The V.I.C. in the book is: _____.

I know this is the very important character because:

1. The character does most of the talking.
2. The character is on almost every page.
3. The character's name is in the title.
4. The character talks to all of the other characters.

This character reminds me of: _____

_____

_____

_____

_____

_____.

3. Strategies for Finding Information: Readers gather, evaluate, and synthesize data and information from a variety of sources.

Page	Mini-Lesson Topic	Literacy Center Connection	Center Title
75	Determining importance in text	Research	"Is It Interesting, Important, or Both?"
79	Gathering information about a topic	Research	"Look and Learn"
83	Skimming and scanning for information in text	Word Work	"Make Me See"
86	Using the classroom environment to locate information	Word Work	"Can You Find It?"

Mini-Lesson: Determining importance in text

Materials: Articles from student magazines and newspapers, "Interesting/Important/Both" sorting
mat (page 77), "What's Important?" student response form (page 78), chart paper
Reader's Workshop Component: Shared Reading

1. Choose an informational article from a student magazine or newspaper.

2. If necessary, make a copy of the article on an overhead so all students have visual access
   to the text.

3. Before reading the text, say: "When I read an informational article, I often find very
   interesting facts in the text. These are the things that make me 'ooh' and 'aah' and 'wow'
   as I read. While this may be interesting information, often it is not the *most* important
   information. Sometimes information is *both* interesting and important. Today, we are
   going to practice listening for what is interesting and what is important."

4. Read the article aloud while the students follow along.

5. After you read, go back and reread a section at a time. Allow students to tell you what
   information is most interesting to them. Then let them tell you the most important part
   about each section. Record their answers on the "Interesting/Important/Both" sorting mat.
   If the fact is both interesting and important, record it in the "both" column of the chart.

6. Explain that it is important to be able to distinguish interesting from important when
   asked to summarize or identify the main idea of a passage.

7. Revisit the chart and ask students to discuss how they made their decisions.

Mini-Lesson Notes

Literacy Center Connection: Research

Center Title: "Is It Interesting, Important, or Both?"

Place several copies of informational magazines and articles in this center along with copies of the "What's Important?" student response form (page 78). Students should read an article and determine the most important information from it. They should also write down some interesting things they learn. Remind students that sometimes information can be *both* interesting and important.

Lesson Variations and Notes

- If possible, use copies of articles that students can highlight and mark as they read.
- For younger students, pre-record several facts from a familiar informational text on index cards. Place a copy of the book in your center for reference. Let students sort the fact cards using the sorting mat from page 77.
- Ask students to complete the student response form on page 78 for assessment.
- The Internet is a great resource to get information for this center.

☑ **Comprehension**
☑ **Fluency**
☐ **Phonemic Awareness**
☐ **Phonics**
☑ **Vocabulary**

Sorting Mat

Interesting	Both	Important

What's Important?

Name: _____ Date: _____

Magazine I Used: _____

Article I Read: _____

Author: _____

Interesting	Both	Important

My thinking:

I chose this article because: _____

_____

_____.

Mini-Lesson: Gathering information about a topic

Materials: Several non-fiction books about the same topic or theme, chart paper and markers, 8½" x 11" paper, envelopes

Reader's Workshop Component: Shared Reading

1. Gather at least four books about the theme or topic you are studying. Divide a piece of chart paper into four sections and label each with a book title you will use for this mini-lesson.
2. Explain to your students that when you want to learn about something specific, you often check several resources.
3. Show your students the books you have chosen and see if they can identify what specific aspect you want them to learn more about. For example, if the books are on the ocean, you could have students specifically focus on whales.
4. Divide your class into four small groups. Give each group a book and ask them to look for sentences or phrases about the topic.
5. As students locate sentences, record them on the chart.
6. Discuss how the information gathered could be used to report on the topic.
7. Post the chart in the Research Center to remind your students how to gather information.

Mini-Lesson Notes

Literacy Center Connection: Research

Center Title: "Look and Learn"

Stock your Research Center with plenty of books on your theme or high-interest topics your students want to study more. Place these books in the center with 8½″ x 11″ paper and tools for writing. Encourage students to make a smaller version of the chart from your mini-lesson using the form on page 81. Make sure they know to cite the book title and page number next to their interesting facts. Students can keep these information sheets in an envelope for reference during the unit of study. See the example on the next page.

Lesson Variations and Notes

- Students can use these information sheets to document their learning in the unit.
- Have students put their facts into a report on the chosen subject.
- Keep blank paper at this center to encourage students to self-select other topics of interest. Collect gift bags with pictures illustrating a specific theme. For example, a bag with fish on it could be used to store informational texts and articles about oceans. Keep these available to encourage re-reading and further investigation.

☑ **Comprehension**
☐ **Fluency**
☐ **Phonemic Awareness**
☐ **Phonics**
☑ **Vocabulary**

Look and Learn

Name:_____   Date:_____

I want to learn more about:_____

Book Title	I learned....	I learned....	I learned...
	page:	page:	page:
	page:	page:	page:
	page:	page:	page:
	page:	page:	page:

This makes me think_____

_____

_____

We want to learn more about: Mountain Animals

Book Title	We learned....	We learned....	We learned...
Bighorn Sheep by JoAnn Early Macken	Bighorns are good at climbing. page: 12	Bighorns grow heavy coats for the winter. page: 20	page:
Cougars by JoAnn Early Macken	A cougar's fur blends in with trees. page: 12	They eat meat. page: 6	They are called Mountain Lions. page: 20
Mountain Goats by JoAnn Early Macken	A baby is called a kid. page: 4	Their feet grip the rocks. page: 14	page:
Elk by JoAnn Early Macken	A group is called a herd. page: 10	Elk eat grass. page: 14	In Spring they move up the mountain. page: 18

This makes me think: Mountain animals have to be good at climbing. They act different in the Spring and Winter. Some animals eat grass and others eat meat.

Mini-Lesson: Skimming and scanning for information in text

Materials: Non-fiction Big Books, newspaper articles (regular or classroom), clipboards, highlighters/highlighting tape, "Make Me See" poster (page 85), "Make Me See" task cards (page 85)

Reader's Workshop Component: Shared Reading

1. Discuss with your students the importance of locating information for a specific purpose. List times when you might need to do this: while reading a phone book, checking a recipe to see if you have the ingredients, looking for sports statistics information on a sports card, finding a word or article in the dictionary or encyclopedia, etc.

2. Say, "Readers must train their eyes to skim and scan text for information. When you look for information in text, you are often looking for something special. For example, if I need to find a friend's phone number, I use my finger to guide my eyes down the page while looking for letters I know are in his name. After I skim the page to find the place I need to focus on, I make my eyes focus a little more until I find the right name."

3. Tell the students they are going to practice skimming and scanning for information using a book or article.

4. Think aloud using the Big Book as a model. Example: "If I want to read about how owls eat and I pick up this book, I skim to see first if it will help me with what I want to know. What special words should I look for?" Help your students understand that they will look for words having to do with food to find this information. Show them how to skim by running your finger quickly over the text.

5. Explain that when you find text that could give you your answer, confirm it with your eyes by scanning the text for the specific information you want. Let students use highlighting tape to show this information.

6. Practice this in several books.

Mini-Lesson Notes

Literacy Center Connection: Word Work

Center Title: "Make Me See"

Display a "Make Me See" poster based on the sheet on page 85 and the task cards on page 85. Provide highlighters and clipboards along with copies of the newspaper. Students check what the "Make Me See" focus is for the week and skim and scan the newspaper to find words, phrases, or sentences that correspond to the weekly focus. When they locate the "Make Me See," they should highlight it. They can write their name on the article and turn it in or keep it in a work folder for you to check later.

Lesson Variation and Notes

- Use a classroom newspaper (such as *Scholastic News, Weekly Reader,* or *Time for Kids*), school newsletters, or morning message for "Make Me See."

- Students can scan science and social studies texts while using removable highlighting tape.

- Students may want to reference highlighted articles during Writing Workshop.

- Call your local textbook depository for surplus and out-of-adoption textbooks students can highlight.

- Younger children can look for information in toy ads or food boxes. It is important for them to have materials that are more colorful and contain less text.

☑ **Comprehension**
☑ **Fluency**
☐ **Phonemic Awareness**
☐ **Phonics**
☑ **Vocabulary**

Make Me See

Directions:

1. Read the types of words to find this week.
2. Select a newspaper article.
3. Use a highlighter to find the types of words that match the ones on the "Make Me See" list.
4. Put your name on the article and place it in the completed folder.

"Make Me See" Task Cards

(to be placed on the "Make Me See" poster)

Who? (People in the article)	**What?** (Tell what happens)
Where? (Places in the article)	**When?** (Days, months, years)
Why? (Show clues to explain why the author wrote this article)	**How?** (Show how the author presents the information)

Words that start with _____
Words that end with _____
Words that rhyme with _____
Words that have the _____ sound
Compound words
Words that have _____ syllables

Mini-Lesson: Using the classroom environment to locate information

Materials: Print displayed around the room, index cards, "Can You Find It?" poster; **Choose one or more of the following:** word frames (envelopes with clear, plastic windows; fly swatter with a hole cut in the center; light switch covers; etc.), pointers, Wikki Stix, highlighting tape

Reader's and /Writer's Workshop Component: Word Work

1. Pre-write cards with letters or words you have been studying in Reader's or Writer's Workshop. Display the "Can You Find It?" poster for your students.

2. Tell students that today, they will be like detectives trying to find special letters or words in the classroom.

3. If students have never used pointers or word frames, model these for them using a Big Book or chart poem.

4. Display a card on the "Can You Find It?" poster. Let children volunteer to find the letter or word indicated. Remind them that many words and letters will be found over and over again in your classroom.

Mini-Lesson Notes

Literacy Center Connection: Word Work

Center Title: "Can You Find It?"

Display the "Can You Find It?" poster in your Word Work Center. Each week, post a letter, letter pattern, word, or word type you are learning during whole- and small-group mini-lessons. Challenge students to locate the posted "Can You Find It?" item in the print around your classroom. For assessment, have them use Wikki Stix, small Post-it notes, or highlighting tape to point out the "Can You Find It?" items around the room, and leave them up at the end of center time. You will quickly be able to see if they were able to locate the "Can You Find It?" item in the context of your classroom.

Lesson Variations and Notes

- Older children can track their "Can You Find It?" exploration on the "Can You Find It?" log on page 88 to record where they found the week's letter or word.

- Laminate your "Can You Find It?" poster. Attach the "Can You Find It?" task cards (below) with Velcro, and stick removable highlighting tape and Wikki Stix to the bottom of the poster for students to use.

- After students have plenty of practice locating the "Can You Find It?" item in the room, challenge them to find it in books.

| ☑ Comprehension |
| ☐ Fluency |
| ☐ Phonemic Awareness |
| ☑ Phonics |
| ☐ Vocabulary |

Possible "Can You Find It?" Task Cards (cut and attach to poster)

Strong verbs	Nouns
Descriptive phrases	Words that start with ____
Color words	Words that end with ____
Comparisons	Words that rhyme with ____
Tricky words (tricky for the reader)	Words that have the _____ sound
Interesting words	Compound words
Words I want to use in my writing	Words that have _____ syllables

Can You Find It?

Name: _____ Date: _____

Here is what I looked for this week: _____

_____

I found...	Here's where I found it...

I noticed... _____

_____.

This helps me know more about:

☐ Reading
☐ Writing
☐ Listening
☐ Viewing
☐ Speaking

4. Strategies for Building Fluency and Independence: Readers self-select appropriate text and read for a variety of purposes.

Page	Mini-Lesson Topic	Literacy Center Connection	Center Title
90	Reading with oral fluency	Poetry	"We've Got the Beat!"
92	Reading and using punctuation	Word Work	"Sentence Sort"
94	Rereading familiar text to build fluency and expression	Literature Response	"Talk to Me"
98	Rereading with a partner to build fluency and expression	Classroom Library	"Book Buddies"

Mini-Lesson: Reading with oral fluency

Materials: Poems written on charts, rhythm sticks (check with your school's music teacher), poetry books, tape player, CDs or cassettes with a variety of beats and rhythms

Reader's Workshop Component: Shared Reading

1. Print any poem your students know on chart paper.

2. Reread the poem with your students during a whole-group lesson.

3. Explain to students that poetry is meant to be read aloud and with rhythm. This makes it more interesting for the reader.

4. Read the poem with a different rhythm than before. Invite your students to clap or use rhythm sticks to keep the beat with you. Encourage them to read along.

5. See if you can vary the rhythm by going faster or slower. After you have modeled this, let your students suggest a beat.

6. Post the poems in the classroom for students to revisit during centers.

Mini-Lesson Notes

Literacy Center Connection: Poetry

Center Title: "We've Got the Beat!"

Place several familiar poems in your Poetry Center. Ask your music teacher to help you record different percussion rhythms and patterns on cassettes or CDs. Store these along with a CD/cassette player in your poetry center for students to try a new rhythm when reading different poems.

Note: Provide a playback pipe made from an elbow of PVC pipe. Children can use the playback pipe to hear their rhythm as they read. (See "14 Ways to Use a Playback Pipe" on page 185 in the Teacher Resources.)

Lesson Variations and Notes

- Many commercial music stores carry CDs and cassettes that have instrumental rhythm music you can use for this center.
- Consider purchasing personal cassette players to allow students to use along with the rhythm cassettes when reading the room. (You may want to research grants available in your area for this purpose.)
- Students can choose a poem from their poetry notebook to read to the beat.
- When printing poems on charts, use two colors to help young children track text.
- Use visual cues and pictures for unknown words on poetry charts.
- Invite school personnel (principal, assistant principal, physical education coach, music teacher, etc.) to read some of your class poems on tapes for students to listen to in the Poetry Center.

☑ **Comprehension**
☑ **Fluency**
☑ **Phonemic Awareness**
☐ **Phonics**
☐ **Vocabulary**

Mini-Lesson: Reading and using punctuation

Materials: Shared or guided reading books, sentences from familiar books printed on tagboard, punctuation sorting cards (see the following page), magnetic tape, metal baking pan

Reader's Workshop Component: Shared or Guided Reading

1. Print sentences without end punctuation from a familiar shared or guided reading book on small tagboard strips. Use sentences with a variety of end punctuation.
2. After reading the book, show students the sentences you have written.
3. Display the punctuation cards on a board or a pocket chart.
4. Ask students to read each sentence with you and decide if it has a period, question mark, or exclamation point at the end.
5. Students can sort the sentences according to the punctuation they think is missing.
6. Provide copies of the text for them to check and confirm their answers.

Mini-Lesson Notes

Literacy Center Connection: Word Work

Center Title: "Sentence Sort"

Divide a metal baking pan into three sections. Place a punctuation card at the top of each section. Prepare strips of several sentences from a familiar text for students to sort. Remember to omit the end punctuation from these sentence strips. Students then practice reading each sentence and decide which punctuation belongs at the end. They will sort each sentence into the appropriate category on the pan. Provide copies of the text for checking. Occasionally, choose sentences from new shared and guided reading books to add to this center.

Storage note: You can store tagboard sentence strips in legal-sized envelopes at this center. Label each envelope with the corresponding book title so students can self-correct.

Lesson Variations and Notes

- Use sentences found in your students' writing samples to put on the strips. Have students pick one with a period, an exclamation point, or a question mark. They can write these on small cards omitting the punctuation. Leave copies of their writing in the center to promote student checking.
- After students sort, have them write two sentences using each type of end punctuation.
- Assess student understanding by having them create one sentence for each type of punctuation.

Sort Cards

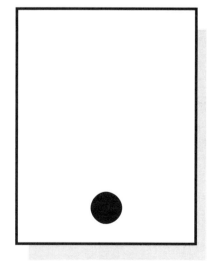  

☑ Comprehension
☑ Fluency
☑ Phonemic Awareness
☐ Phonics
☐ Vocabulary

Mini-Lesson: Rereading familiar text to build fluency and expression

Materials: Familiar text, dialogue cards, prop boxes, highlighters
Reader's Workshop Component: Shared Reading

1. Select a familiar Big Book with dialogue written in color, highlighted with highlighting tape, or duplicated on an overhead transparency.

2. Begin modeling the dialogue between two characters with a think-aloud: "Sometimes I get confused when I am reading books that have many characters talking. This talking between characters is called dialogue. When I read this dialogue, I try to talk the way the characters would. This helps me understand the story better because I can imagine the characters talking. For example, [show one sentence from a Big Book or transparency]. This character in the story feels [excited, sad, scared, etc.], so when I read the dialogue it should sound like this: [use voice inflections to model the character talking]. I might even make my face look like this while I read to look more like the character [use body language]. I could even use props from the prop box to act out my part."

3. Divide the class into pairs. Copy the speech bubble on page 96. Fill them with dialogue from the story. Give each pair of students a set of speech bubbles. Have them practice their scene together using voice, body language, and/or props (see page 97 for prop ideas).

4. Let pairs share out loud with the rest of the class.

Mini-Lesson Notes

Literacy Center Connection: Literature Response

Center Title: "Talk to Me"

Students can build fluency by practicing dialogue from familiar text. Use the speech bubble pattern on page 96 to write out simple dialogue between two characters. Make copies of the filled-in bubbles, cut them out, and place them at the center. If there are more than two characters, make additional cards. Students then work with a partner to read their dialogue with fluency and expression. The goal is to re-create a scene from the story. Encourage students to use body language, voice, and props when appropriate. Occasionally, invite students to share their scenes with small groups or the entire class.

Lesson Variations and Notes

- Copy speech bubbles on different-colored paper. Number the cards to order the dialogue. Older students can write out their own dialogue or highlight their part with different-colored markers.

- Set up a prop box in the center to assist the readers. Some students will feel more comfortable using puppets or stuffed animals as they act out the stories. Simple and inexpensive puppets can be made by removing the stuffing from a stuffed animal.

- Start off prop boxes with only a few items that are relevant to the story. The goal is to encourage students to reread for fluency. Add props as you add more stories to the center.

- Select appropriate text levels and teaching points during the modeling stage. Draw attention to features of dialogue such as quotation marks, speech bubbles, italics, text color, etc. Have students highlight words that indicate expression such as "said," "replied," "shouted," "cried," "exclaimed," etc.

- Store the book and dialogue cards in a large manila envelope for easy access and cleanup.

☑ Comprehension
☑ Fluency
☑ Phonemic Awareness
☐ Phonics
☐ Vocabulary

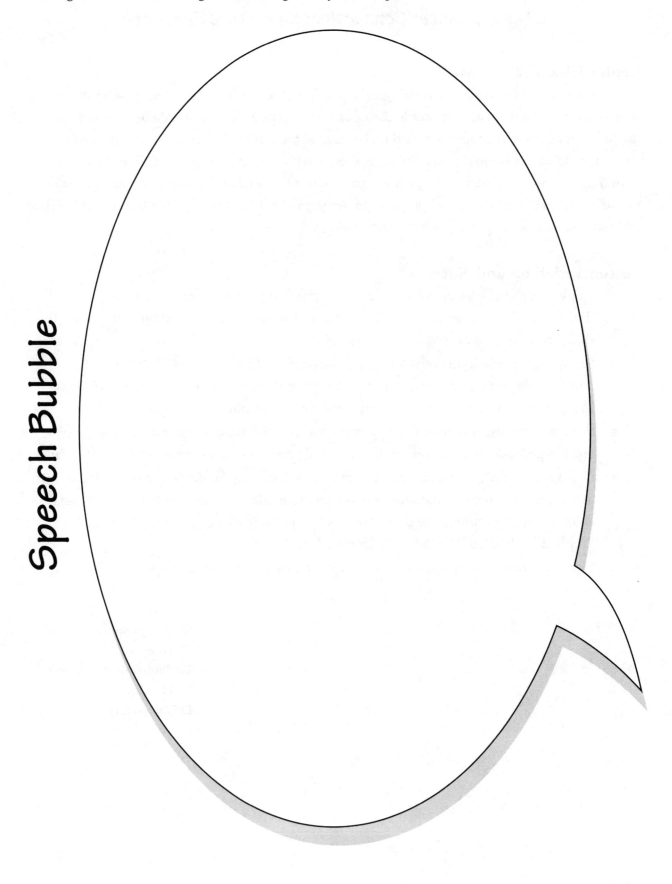

Speech Bubble

Prop Ideas for Your Classroom

Item	Use it for...
Assorted cloth pieces	Clothing, flags, boundaries for buildings or rooms, beds
Bandana	Skirt, hat, tie, shawl, tablecloth, picnic blanket
Basket	Picnic basket, fishing tackle box, purse, baby cradle, bassinet, shopping basket
Dowel rod	Fishing pole, cane, magic wand, microphone
Gloves	Puppets, motorcycle gear, surgical gloves
Large sponges	Walls, phones, cars, pathways
Lunch box	Fishing tackle box, tool box, typewriter, briefcase, luggage
Plastic plate	Steering wheel, food tray, plate
Section of garden hose	Fire hose, rope
Streamer	Caution tape, party decorations, skirts, flowers
Towel	Bed, couch, skirt, cape, hood, baby blanket
Wooden spoons	Puppets, microphone, magic wand, pointer

©2006 Nations & Alonso, *More Primary Literacy Centers*

Mini-Lesson: Rereading with a partner to build fluency and expression

Materials: Basket of familiar books, "Book Buddies" manners chart (page 100), transparency and class copies of "Book Buddies" form (page 101)

Reader's Workshop Component: Independent Reading

1. Select a student to help you model "Book Buddies" manners. Begin with a think-aloud: "Today I am going to share one of my favorite books with a buddy. This is a book I have read many times before, and I can't wait to read it to [insert name]. Before I begin reading, I want to make sure that my buddy and I practice good "Book Buddies" manners. This will help us listen to and enjoy the story.

2. Display the "Book Buddies" manners chart from page 100 for the entire class to view. Model each step with a student.

3. Have students select a familiar text they have been reading independently, and pair up each student with a buddy.

4. Provide practice time for reading and listening. Walk around and monitor book buddies, providing feedback to encourage good manners.

5. Model how to complete a "Book Buddies" form (page 101) on the overhead projector. Have students complete their own forms.

Mini-Lesson Notes

Literacy Center Connection: Classroom Library

Center Title: "Book Buddies"

Copy and laminate the "Book Buddies" manners chart on page 100. Place several copies of familiar texts in a basket at this center. Add pillows or beanbag chairs to create a comfortable seating area. Have students reread a familiar text with a buddy. Remind students to practice "Book Buddies" manners when they are reading and/or listening to their partners. After the reading, have students complete the "Book Buddies" form on page 101 and place it in their center folder. (Note: An additional "Book Buddies" reading log, titled "My Weekly Buddy Reading Record," is included in the Teacher Resources on page 186.)

Lesson Variations and Notes

- Model a variety of lessons over time using a picture book, a section of an informational text, a poem, published student writing, etc.

- Display the "Book Buddies" manners chart so that it is clearly visible to students. Options might include: laminated sentence strips attached by a key ring, written on a large chart, poster with photos of the students practicing good manners, etc.

- Use the "Book Buddies" forms as a conferencing tool with individual readers.

☑ **Comprehension**
☑ **Fluency**
☐ **Phonemic Awareness**
☐ **Phonics**
☑ **Vocabulary**

"Book Buddies" Manners

Everyone:

1. Choose a book that you have read.

2. Pick the part you want to read to your buddy.

3. Sit next to your book buddy in a quiet place.

4. Decide who will read first.

Readers:

1. Tell your buddy the name of your book.

2. Read loud enough for your buddy to hear.

3. Let your buddy look at the book with you.

4. Ask your buddy for help if you need it.

Listeners:

1. Listen quietly.

2. Look at the book while your buddy reads.

3. Think about what you like.

4. Help your buddy if he or she asks you.

Book Buddies

Reader's Name: _____

Listener's Name: _____

Book Title: _____

Reader:

I read _____ A book _____ A poem _____ My own writing

One thing I liked about reading was _____

_____

_____.

One thing I learned about my reading was _____

_____

_____.

Listener:

I heard _____ A book _____ A poem _____ A buddy's writing

One thing I liked about listening was _____

_____

_____ _____

_____.

Chapter Eight
Writing Connections

1.	**Strategies for Word Choice:** Writers use their understandings of words and their meaning to make effective word choices.
2.	**Strategies for Using Information:** Writers communicate their discoveries for a variety of purposes and audiences.
3.	**Strategies for Communicating a Message:** Writers construct text for a variety of purposes.
4.	**Strategies for Building Fluency and Independence:** Writers self-select topics and write for a variety of purposes.

1. Strategies for Word Choice: Writers use their understanding of words and their meanings to make effective word choices.

Page	Mini-Lesson Topic	Literacy Center Connection	Center Title
103	Using sound/symbol relationships to identify and make new words	Word Work	"Stamp It Out"
105	Using resources to make word choices in writing	Writing	"Mini-Dictionaries"
109	Practicing word choice through poetry innovation	Poetry	"Innovation Station"
111	Using print resources to identify words to improve writing	Writing	"Write the Room"

Mini-Lesson: Using sound/symbol relationships to identify and make new words

Materials: Rubber stamps with upper- and lowercase letters, washable ink stamp pads (available at the local art supply store), baby wipes for cleanup, chart paper, markers and crayons

Writer's Workshop Component: Guided Writing

1. Say: "Sometimes when I am writing, I don't know how to spell a word. I have to stop and think about the sounds I hear. One trick that helps me is to say the word very slowly and think about each sound I hear. I write down each letter as I think about it."

2. Explain to your students that they will be helping you make words by using rubber stamps.

3. Choose a list of words you would like students to make.

4. Begin by saying the first word. Ask, "Who hears the first sound in _____?" When a student identifies a sound, let her come up and stamp it on the chart paper in its correct location. Then ask, "Who hears the next sound in _____?" Continue until the entire word has been spelled out on the chart paper. Help students read it slowly so they can hear the segmented sounds. Then read it fast so they can think about how it would sound in context.

5. Continue in this manner until you have made several words.

6. Review the list with your students.

7. Display the list in the room for students to read and reference during readers' and writers' workshop.

Mini-Lesson Notes

Literacy Center Connection: Word Work

Center Title: "Stamp It Out"

Place the alphabet stamps in your Word Work Center. Talk to students about how to care for this center prior to letting them use it. Encourage them to stamp words they know, word families, and any other interesting words they discover. You can keep a card with your stamps that tells students what they will need to stamp out. For example, "Stamp It Out: Words that sound like <u>mat</u>." Change the words regularly to maintain student interest and develop further word attack skills.

Words that sound like:

m a t

___ ___ ___

___ ___ ___

___ ___ ___

___ ___ ___

Lesson Variations and Notes

- Store rubber stamps in fishing tackle boxes labeled with corresponding letters.
- Occasionally have students help wipe the stamps off with baby wipes. This will preserve your stamps for a long time.
- Students will enjoy the challenge of stamping out whole sentences. Write sentences out on small strips of paper for them to reproduce using the rubber stamps.
- With the youngest learners, have them begin by stamping out their friends' names. Keep a class name list at this center for student reference.

☐ **Comprehension**
☐ **Fluency**
☑ **Phonemic Awareness**
☑ **Phonics**
☑ **Vocabulary**

Mini-Lesson: Using resources to make word choices in writing

Materials: Sentence strips; stickers, clip art, and/or small photos; binding combs or book rings; "Check Three, Then Me" poster (page 107); "Check Three, Then Me" tickets (page 108); "Try It Out Log" (page 187 in the Teacher Resources); chart paper; markers

Writer's Workshop Component: Shared Writing

1. Help students see that sometimes writers don't know how to spell a word when they write. Use a think-aloud such as, "When I write, there are times I don't know how to spell a word I am trying to use. When this happens, there are many things I can do. I can stop and look it up, but I don't want to forget what I am trying to say. So, I write all the letters I hear in the word, circle it, and keep writing. The circle reminds me to come back later and find the correct spelling of the word."

2. Continue with, "When I come back to words I circled, I can check the spelling in many ways. I can ask someone. I can look for the word somewhere else, like in a dictionary or in the spell-check on my computer. What else can I do?"

3. Generate a list with your students of places they can look in the classroom to check the spelling of unknown words.

4. Students often ask the teacher as a first strategy. To encourage them to become more independent, post a sign reminding them to "Check Three, Then Me". Keep the list of options for checking spelling posted in your classroom.

5. For additional reinforcement, students can use the tickets to show you what three sources they checked for spelling before asking the teacher.

Mini-Lesson Notes

Literacy Center Connection: Writing

Center Title: "Mini-Dictionaries"

Use clip art from your old workbooks, stickers, and magazine pictures to create mini-dictionaries. Attach the pictures to a small sentence strip or index card with the word written on it. These mini-dictionaries are a nice addition to thematic units you may be doing in class. After you collect ten to twelve pictures in a category, laminate the cards and attach them using a binding machine or a key ring.

As you add mini-dictionaries to your Writing Center, be sure to share them with the whole class so they know what is available. Students can use these mini-dictionaries when they are looking for words to use in their writing.

Lesson Variations and Notes

- Provide mini-dictionaries at your Writing Center to be used all year long. Begin by making one using a copy of a photograph of each of your students. The first dictionary can be called, "My Classmates' Names."
- Store these dictionaries in a small shoebox or container labeled "Mini-Dictionaries."
- Highlight anchor words on your word wall to help kids spell using analogies. For example, if I can spell "look," then I can spell "book," "hook," "took," etc.
- Provide each child with a highlighter for choosing five words they want to spell-check in their own writing.
- A "Try-It-Out Log" is available in the Teacher Resources on page 187 for students to record spelling strategies they use when writing.

☐	Comprehension
☐	Fluency
☐	Phonemic Awareness
☑	Phonics
☑	Vocabulary

When you don't know a word…

Check three:

Word Wall

A	B	C
are ask	be bye	can ask
D	**E**	**F**
do did does	each	for found

Ask a Friend

Look in the dictionary

Dictionary

Then ask me!

Check Three Then Me Tickets

My Name:_____
I checked

☐ Word Wall

☐ My Friend

☐ Dictionary

My Name:_____
I checked

☐ Word Wall

☐ My Friend

☐ Dictionary

My Name:_____
I checked

☐ Word Wall

☐ My Friend

☐ Dictionary

My Name:_____
I checked

☐ Word Wall

☐ My Friend

☐ Dictionary

My Name:_____
I checked

☐ Word Wall

☐ My Friend

☐ Dictionary

My Name:_____
I checked

☐ Word Wall

☐ My Friend

☐ Dictionary

My Name:_____
I checked

☐ Word Wall

☐ My Friend

☐ Dictionary

My Name:_____
I checked

☐ Word Wall

☐ My Friend

☐ Dictionary

My Name:_____
I checked

☐ Word Wall

☐ My Friend

☐ Dictionary

My Name:_____
I checked

☐ Word Wall

☐ My Friend

☐ Dictionary

Mini-Lesson: Practicing word choice through poetry innovation

Materials: Familiar poem chart, sticky notes, markers
Writer's Workshop Component: Shared Writing

1. Display a familiar poem on chart paper or the overhead. Reread and enjoy.

2. Cover up key words with sticky notes.

3. Do a think-aloud: "When I change the words of this poem, it changes the meaning. When I read, it's important to get a clear picture in my head. This helps me to better understand what I am reading. When I choose new words for a poem, I have to make sure they will make sense to the reader and me. I also need to make sure that I keep the rhythm and rhyme of the poem in mind."

4. Invite students to brainstorm new words. Place them in the text and reread. Try out several possibilities before settling on one.

5. Discuss similarities and differences between the two poems.

6. Let students practice innovating a familiar poem with a partner or in a small group.

Mini-Lesson Notes

Literacy Center Connection: Poetry

Center Title: "Innovation Station"

Type familiar poems on 8½" x 11" paper with key words omitted. Laminate for durability. Provide a word list at the center so young students can choose a word instead of having to think one up without a model. Students can select new words for the poem and fill in the blanks. They can use sticky notes, dry erase markers or write on their own personal copy. Students can share their new poems with a partner. You may want to have students put their poems into a poetry notebook and write a response (see page 122).

Lesson Variations and Notes

- Begin with nursery rhymes and delete only a few words for younger students. Pre-select new word possibilities with the poem for students to use in their innovation.

- Select a focus for older readers. Coordinate the poem deletions with practice for parts of speech. Delete verbs and model how to innovate a poem using strong verbs. Delete adjectives and model specific word choice.

- Innovate favorite songs.

- Publish poetry innovations and place them in the Classroom Library or Writing Center.

- Add a playback pipe for students to practice rereading their innovations.

☑	**Comprehension**
☑	**Fluency**
☑	**Phonemic Awareness**
☑	**Phonics**
☑	**Vocabulary**

Mini-Lesson: Using print resources to identify words to improve writing

Materials: Chart paper, markers, highlighters, print resources, transparency of "Write the Room" recording sheet (page 114)

Writer's Workshop Component: Shared Writing

1. Begin with a think-aloud: "Good writers know how to use specific words in their writing. When they can't think of words on their own, good writers know where to find words they can use. They also know how to check words for meaning and spelling. When I look around our room, I see many places to find words I need."

2. Generate a list with the students of places around the room to find words. These may include: word walls, charts, dictionaries, poems, books, word lists, writing folders, etc.

3. Explain to students that they will practice locating and recording words from around your room. Display a sentence strip with this week's "Write the Room" focus (a specific prefix, suffix, sound, etc.). For example, "Find words with an -ing ending."

4. Model how to use the print resources in the room to find words ending with -ing.

5. Place the "Write the Room" recording sheet from page 114 on the overhead, and write the words students find. Highlight the -ing ending in each word.

6. Reread the list. Circle the words you want students to use in their writing this week.

Mini-Lesson Notes

Literacy Center Connection: Writing

Center Title: "Write the Room"

Post the "Write the Room" directions from page 113 in the Writing Center. Provide clipboards, highlighters, and the "Write the Room" recording sheet from page 114. Students can use a variety of print resources, such as the word wall, charts, books, dictionaries, etc., to find words with this week's focus. Students write the words on the recording sheet and use highlighters to identify specific word parts, writer's crafts, or words they want to remember for their own writing.

Lesson Variations and Notes

- Students may generate a class list of topics they could use for "Write the Room."
- Instead of clipboards, give each student a "Write the Room" notebook to keep as a reference for writing.
- Vary the level of difficulty by selecting three different targets: easy to find, harder to find, and very challenging to find.
- Possible "Write the Room" Topics:
    o Words that begin with _____
    o Words that end with _____
    o Words that rhyme with _____
    o Color words
    o Nouns
    o Strong verbs
    o Compound words
    o Interesting words
    o Describing words

☑ **Comprehension**
☑ **Fluency**
☑ **Phonemic Awareness**
☑ **Phonics**
☑ **Vocabulary**

"Write the Room" Directions

1. Use a clipboard.

2. Look for this:

3. Write.

"Write the Room" Recording Sheet

Name: _____

I am looking for:

2. Strategies for Using Information: Writers communicate their discoveries for a variety of purposes and audiences.

Page	Mini-Lesson Topic	Literacy Center Connection	Center Title
116	Recording information learned in text	Literature Response	"WOW!"
118	Recording observations using descriptive details	Research	"What Do You Notice?"
122	Using information from poetry to generate a response	Poetry	"Poetry Place"
126	Using information from stories to create a product	Listening	"Make a Menu"

Mini-Lesson: Recording information learned in text

Materials: Construction paper cut in half lengthwise (12" x 18" cut to 6" x 18"), large die-cut letters to spell "WOW" (white is best), glue, markers or colored pencils

Writing Workshop Component: Independent Writing

1. Provide each student with multiple copies of a variety of familiar informational texts to read.

2. Say, "When I read informational text, I usually find some facts or information that make me say 'Wow!' Today we are going to look at this book and see if you can find some interesting facts or information." Let students spend a few minutes with the text looking for an interesting fact or piece of information. They should raise their hands when they find something that makes them say, "Wow!"

3. Let students share their "WOW" with a partner. Talk about what happens when someone shares interesting parts of a book. Did it make them want to read their partner's book? Why?

4. Let students trade books and look for more "WOWs." They should continue sharing with their partner as they find things that interest them.

5. Display a blank 6" x 18" sheet of construction paper. Show the students the die-cut letters to spell "WOW." Glue the letters on your construction paper and explain that the students are going to create a "WOW" sheet with the information they found in one book.

6. Demonstrate how to write information inside the letters using a book you read. One color per fact makes them easier to read.

7. Students should record the book title on the top of the "WOW" sheet. Display these in your Research Center.

Mini-Lesson Notes

Literacy Center Connection: Literature Response

Center Title: "WOW!"

Students should select a book from your classroom collection of informational texts. Pre-cut the large letters to spell "WOW." Students can cut a sheet of construction paper in half lengthwise and glue down the letters. They should record the title of the book where they located information. Then they should write down two interesting facts per letter in "WOW." Display these in the Research Center for further investigation or to spark interest in your informational text collection.

(Note: The "Literacy Response Chart with Explanations" found in the Teacher Resources can be used with this center.)

Lesson Variation and Notes

- Use as an assessment tool by having all your students record from the same text.
- Let students try this with poetry and record phrases or words that make them say, "Wow!"
- Bind the "WOW" sheets into a book for browsing in the Classroom Library.
- Store the "WOW" letters in a baby wipes container or shoebox labeled "WOW" for student access at this center.

☑ **Comprehension**
☐ **Fluency**
☐ **Phonemic Awareness**
☐ **Phonics**
☑ **Vocabulary**

Mini-Lesson: Recording observations using descriptive details

Materials: Properties Chart (page 120), Properties Observation Sheet (page 121), overhead transparency of properties observation sheet, magnifying glass, balance scale, pencils

Writer's Workshop Component: Interactive Writing

1. Bring in an interesting object, such as a bug, to observe together.
2. Sit children with you in a group. Think aloud about what you notice. Say, "When I look at this bug, I notice many things. I notice it is black with brown spots. I see it has six legs. It is smaller than a frog. The bug is shaped like an oval."
3. Help children understand that when you observe something closely and notice its properties, you are like a scientist. Explain that scientists record their observations. Say, "Today we are going to record our observations."
4. Display the properties chart titled "What Do You Notice?"
5. Record your observations together. Have children help you write the information on the overhead transparency.
6. Remind students that good writers include details in their writing. This helps the reader understand and visualize what the writing is about.

Mini-Lesson Notes

Literacy Center Connection: Research Center

Center Title: "What Do You Notice?"

In your Research Center, display a large version of the properties chart shown on page 120. Each week, display a new object such as a bug, shell, rock, and other items of interest for students to observe. They can use the properties observation sheet on page 121 to record what they notice about the object of the week. Remind them that scientists are always noticing the world around them. They often record what they notice and begin to ask questions based on their observations. Encourage students to do further investigations on other topics of interest.

Lesson Variations and Notes

- You might want to check out the series, *Thinking Like a Scientist*, available from Newbridge Educational Publishing. These Big Books are a nice way to show children the scientific process of inquiry.
- For added authenticity, provide children with lab coats made from old white dress shirts, glasses, and clipboards for recording information.
- Place a basket of non-fiction books and articles about the week's observation item in the center to encourage further investigation.
- Purchase inexpensive, personal tape recorders for students to discuss their observations and use later in Writing Workshop.

☑ **Comprehension**
☑ **Fluency**
☐ **Phonemic Awareness**
☐ **Phonics**
☑ **Vocabulary**

From Susan: In Kristin Boerger's kindergarten classroom, students begin this center during the first two weeks of school. She keeps picture books with one word per page at this center for students to use as a reference when they write about an object. For example, if students begin by observing marbles, they can find the page in the book with a photo of marbles and the matching word. Initially, she only posts one property, such as color, on her chart. She encourages students to write the color or colors of the object they observe, try to write the name, and then draw a picture. Gradually, she adds more properties to the chart and invites students to begin writing in more detail about their observations.

Properties Chart

Color:

- ○ Red
- ○ Orange
- ○ Yellow
- ○ Green
- ○ Purple
- ○ Black
- ○ White
- ○ Brown

Weight:

Light

Medium

Heavy

Shape:

Circle

Oval

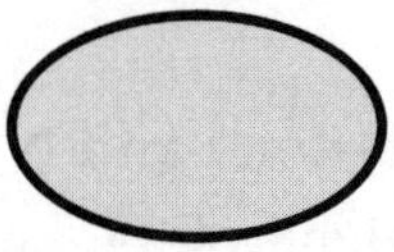

Rectangle

Square

Triangle

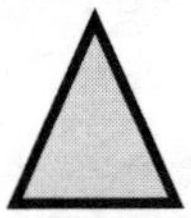

Hexagon

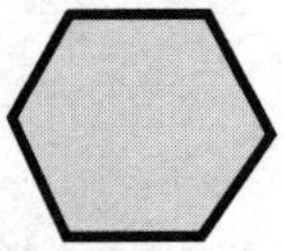

Octagon

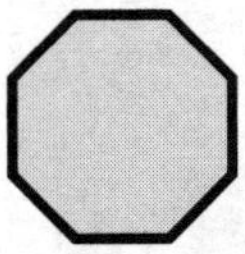

Rhombus

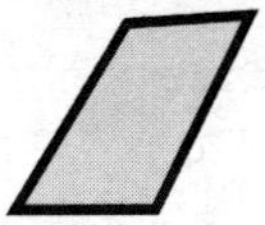

My Observation Form

Scientist: _____ Date: _____

Object Observed: _____

My Picture:

I noticed:

Color: _____ Shape: _____

Size: _____ Weight: _____

Mini-Lesson: Using information from poetry to generate a response

Materials: Copies of a featured poem, highlighters, poetry notebooks, "Poetry Place" response stems (page 125)

Writer's Workshop Component: Modeled Writing

1. Display a poem on a large chart or overhead transparency. Be sure all students have visual access to the text.

2. Read the poem with your students and display the response stem, "This poem reminds me of..." (I like to launch this lesson with "Sick" by Shel Silverstein.) Say, "When I read this poem, it reminds me of a time when I was so tired that I didn't want to go to school. I tried to make excuses about being sick, but my mom didn't believe me. I can write about this connection in my journal to help me better understand this poem."

3. Write two to three sentences on the overhead about your personal connection to the poem. Use examples from the poem in your connection as you write (see example below).

"Sick" by Shel Silverstein reminds me of the time when I was nine and I didn't want to go to school. I told my Mom I had a sore throat. She told me if I was really sick, I couldn't go to the movies the next day. I got up and got dressed just like Sally did in the poem.

Mini-Lesson Notes

Literacy Center Connection: Poetry

Center Title: "Poetry Place"

Place copies of this week's featured poem in the Poetry Center. Have students cut out the poem and glue or tape it to the left side of their poetry notebooks. On the right side, have students write a response about the poem. Student responses should be written in complete sentences and include information from the poem. Younger students might draw and write simple sentences as their response. You can post the "Poetry Place" directions on page 124 for your students.

Lesson Variations and Notes

- Display several written responses in the center to serve as models.
- Informational poems are a wonderful source of facts written in a different genre. Have students read these poems and list facts they learned.
- Keep a playback pipe at the center for students to practice reading the poems prior to writing.
- Response stem ideas can be found on page 125.
- Provide highlighters at the center for students to highlight important information in the poem they want to discuss in their responses.
- Poetry notebooks are just one way to store responses. Students can complete a response and place it in their center folder for assessment and feedback.

☑ Comprehension
☑ Fluency
☑ Phonemic Awareness
☑ Phonics
☑ Vocabulary

Poetry Place Directions

1. Find this week's poem.

2. Cut it out and glue it to your notebook.

3. Draw and write what you think, feel, or remember.

4. Practice reading the poem.

5. Share it with a friend.

6. Put your Poetry Notebook away.

Poetry Place Response Stems

This poem reminds me of...

Interesting words were...

Facts I learned are...

_____ is a good

title because...

Questions I have are...

Mini-Lesson: Using information from stories to create a product

Materials: Chart paper, food coupons with pictures of food items, markers, familiar folktale
Writer's Workshop Component: Shared Writing

1. Reread a familiar version of a folktale starring the Big Bad Wolf. There are several different stories that could be used for this lesson: *Little Red Riding Hood, The Three Pigs, The True Story of the 3 Little Pigs,* etc.

2. Discuss how hungry the Big Bad Wolf was and say, "When I think about the Big Bad Wolf, I can't help but wonder if we made a delicious menu for him, maybe he would leave those three little pigs alone!"

3. Give pairs of students several food coupons to design a menu that might be tasty to the Big Bad Wolf.

4. Create a class menu on chart paper. Have students label the menus and create prices.

5. Post this chart near your Listening Center for students to use when they make their own menus.

Mini-Lesson Notes

Literacy Center Connection: Listening

Center Title: "Make a Menu"

In addition to books with read-aloud cassettes, stock this center with food coupons, construction paper, glue, and scissors. Invite students to think about a book they just heard at the Listening Center and create a menu for one of the characters in that book. Display several simple menus from local restaurants as models for the students. Have students glue or draw pictures of food items, label, and create prices. See page 128 for sample menu items from familiar folktales, fairy tales, or nursery rhymes.

Lesson Variations and Notes

- Older students can write detailed descriptions of each menu item they select. For example, an item for the Big Bad Wolf might be "Pigs in a Blanket: A delicious hot dog wrapped in a warm, golden biscuit."
- Completed menus can be displayed and used in a Dramatic Play Center or Art Center.
- Students can role-play the characters as they order from the menu.
- Students can write commercials for their restaurants and act them out in a readers' theater. For more information on readers' theater, see *The Fluent Reader* by Timothy Rasinski (Scholastic Professional Books, 2003).

☐ **Comprehension**
☐ **Fluency**
☐ **Phonemic Awareness**
☑ **Phonics**
☑ **Vocabulary**

Make a Menu

The Three Bears' Breakfast
Biscuits and honey
Fresh berries
Oatmeal
Juice

Humpty Dumpty's Brunch
Egg-free omelet
Toast with butter
Tea

Johnny Appleseed's Dessert Land
Apple pie
Apple turnovers
Apple dumplings
Apple juice

Hansel and Gretel's Candy Shop
Gumdrops
Fruit rolls
Candy canes
Icing
Cakes and cookies

Peter Rabbit's Salad Bar
Lettuce
Cabbage
Tomatoes
Carrots
Dressing

Snow White's Fruit Stand
Oranges
Plums
Peaches
Grapes
This location is very far from Johnny Appleseed's Dessert Land

3. Strategies for Communicating a Message: Writers construct text for a variety of purposes.

Page	Mini-Lesson Topic	Literacy Center Connection	Center Title
130	Writing steps in a process	Research	"Build It Up!"
132	Writing to persuade	Classroom Library	"Book Brag"
134	Writing in response to reading	Classroom Library	"Making Connections"
136	Creating an authentic purpose to communicate through writing	Writing	"Tell the Teacher"

Mini-Lesson: Writing steps in a process

Materials: Blocks or other building materials, chart paper or overhead projector
Writers' Workshop Component: Shared Writing

1. Ask, "How many of you have ever read a recipe?" Have your students explain to you what a recipe is and how it helps you when you cook. They should discuss how a recipe is a process or directions for making something.

2. Say, "I notice that many of you can make some pretty neat things with our blocks [or your chosen material]. I wonder if you could give a friend directions to make a building you have made. Let's practice with our talking."

3. Pair students up and give each pair a file folder to hide a building behind. Let one child build a simple structure with blocks that cannot be seen by the partner.

4. After the building is complete, have the builder give directions and describe the building to her partner to see if he can duplicate it.

5. Let the other partner have a turn building and giving the instructions. Talk about how hard (or easy) it was to duplicate something you could not see. Why? You may want to discuss how important transition words, such as first, next, then, and finally, are when listing a sequence of events or set of directions.

6. Consider how hard it is for a recipe writer to write the directions. They must think about each step in the process.

7. You might consider reading *Peanut Butter and Jelly: A Play Rhyme* by Nadine Bernard Westcott (Puffin Books, 1992) as a follow-up to this mini-lesson.

Mini-Lesson Notes

Literacy Center Connection: Research

Center Title: "Build It Up!"

Place several different types of construction materials, such as blocks, tinker toys, or other interlocking materials, in your Research Center. Students can build a structure and then write directions to explain how to make it. They should read their writing to a friend and see if he or she can reconstruct the structure. Younger children should use pictures to re-create their building. Bind some of the directions together in a book called "Build It Up!" for students to practice reading and following directions.

Lesson Variations and Notes

- Invite a parent to help children make a recipe. They should verbally talk about the steps in the process. When the cooking experience is over, have the students try to write their own recipes.
- This center can also be done with art projects. Change the building materials to art supplies such as construction paper scraps, scissors, glue, markers, etc. Students can give directions to complete a puppet or a picture.
- Take photos of your students' creations. They can match the photo with the description.

From Susan: When working in a second-grade classroom, I enjoyed seeing students take this activity to another level by creating a simple step book. Each step of the book contained written directions and diagrams for making their buildings. Students kept their step books in a basket at this center for their peers to try out.

☑ Comprehension
☑ Fluency
☐ Phonemic Awareness
☐ Phonics
☐ Vocabulary

Mini-Lesson: Writing to persuade

Materials: Several read-aloud and shared reading titles, magazine advertisements, classroom book order forms, poster board or large construction paper, markers

Writer's Workshop Component: Shared Writing

1. Ask, "Have you ever seen a commercial on television? Why are they on during shows?"

2. Help children understand that commercials are trying to persuade the viewer to buy or use a product.

3. Show some magazine advertisements and discuss their purpose.

4. Say, "Magazine and television advertisements are written by an author or a group of authors. They try to think of ways to get you to buy or use a product." Look at some of the words that are used in the magazine ads. You may also want to use your classroom book order forms to point out persuasive words. Create a chart of these words for students to use in their writing.

5. Invite students to try some classroom advertising. Show them several read-aloud books and ask for ideas for advertisements that would get others to read them.

6. Have each child pick one title and create an advertisement poster. Explain that students can use pictures, but they must also use words to help the reader choose this book.

7. As children create their posters, conference with them about their choices of words and how they will communicate with their audience.

Mini-Lesson Notes

Literacy Center Connection: Classroom Library

Center Title: "Book Brag"

Place a basket with poster paper and markers in your Classroom Library. When your students finish reading a good book, they can create a poster to "brag" about it. Provide a space, such as a bulletin board, or create a big book to display the "Book Brag" posters for students to use when selecting books. Keep this center fresh by having students create a new "Book Brag" each month.

Lesson Variations and Notes

- When you take the "Book Brag" posters down from the bulletin board, bind them into a big book for students to use in your Classroom Library.
- Use the "Book Brag" poster to assess descriptive writing skills. Before you have students begin writing, explain to them that they will need to have a specific description (i.e., comparison) in their posters.
- Have students present their posters orally as a book commercial.
- Talk to your school media specialist about displaying the posters in the media center to be shared with the whole school.

☑ **Comprehension**
☑ **Fluency**
☐ **Phonemic Awareness**
☐ **Phonics**
☑ **Vocabulary**

Mini-Lesson: Writing in response to reading

Materials: Large piece of bulletin-board paper, several picture books, chart paper and markers, large sticky notes or index cards

Writer's Workshop Component: Modeled Writing

1. Begin with a think-aloud: When I read a book, it often reminds me of something I have seen or done before. This is called making a connection. Good readers think about connections they can make when they read. Making and thinking about connections helps the reader understand the book better."

2. Select a section of a familiar book to read aloud to your students. Model for them how you connect to this story.

3. Say, "Sometimes we want to write about our connections. A written connection needs to clearly explain what the text makes you think, feel, or remember. Let's brainstorm some ways to start a sentence to explain a connection."

4. Help students brainstorm some of the following sentence-starters. List them on a chart and post them in your Classroom Library.

   > This reminds me of…
   >
   > This makes me think about…
   >
   > I remember when…
   >
   > I feel that…

5. Select one of the sentence stems to model your own connection writing.

6. Explain to students that they will have the opportunity to practice making connections when they visit the Classroom Library.

Mini-Lesson Notes

Literacy Center Connection: Classroom Library

Center Title: "Making Connections"

Display a large piece of bulletin-board paper or poster board in your Classroom Library. Also, display the poster you created during the modeled writing lesson for reference. Make sure students have access to markers, colored pencils, and/or sticky notes to record their connections. Students can add their connections to the bulletin board (almost graffiti-style) in this center. Occasionally, visit this chart or poster board to see what connections students are making in their reading.

Lesson Variations and Notes

- Create a smaller version of your connection chart and put it in the front of each student's literature response log.

- Consider using a smaller version students can take home and use to make connections with their parents or another significant adult reader.

- For more information on making connections, read *Mosaic of Thought* by Ellin Oliver Keene and Susan Zimmerman (Heinemann, 1997) and *Reading with Meaning* by Debbie Miller (Stenhouse Publishers, 2002).

□ Comprehension
□ Fluency
□ Phonemic Awareness
☑ Phonics
☑ Vocabulary

Mini-Lesson: Creating an authentic purpose to communicate through writing

Materials: Notebook titled "Tell the Teacher," blank transparency
Writer's Workshop Component: Modeled Writing

1. Begin with a think-aloud: "Sometimes you might have a suggestion you want to share with me to help our classroom run more smoothly. We are going to start collecting your ideas in a notebook called "Tell the Teacher." When I want someone to listen to what I have to say, I need to think carefully about the words I choose and how they sound. For example, I have noticed that the marker caps are not always snapped on the markers. This is a problem for other people who want to use the markers because they might dry out. I need to write a suggestion to help solve this problem."

2. Model writing a problem with a suggested solution on an overhead transparency.

3. Introduce the spiral notebook titled "Tell the Teacher." Explain to students that they may visit this notebook during center time to record their problems and suggestions for your classroom community. Remind students that this is *not* a place to tattle.

4. Tell students how often you will check the notebook and share ideas with the class.

Mini-Lesson Notes

Literacy Center Connection: Writing

Center Title: "Tell the Teacher"
Display the "Tell the Teacher" notebook in the center. Invite students to write classroom suggestions, questions, and/or solutions to problems in this notebook. Select appropriate pages to read aloud to the class during a community meeting. This will provide students with a real purpose for writing and let them feel that their voices are heard in the classroom.

Lesson Variations and Notes
- Use a suggestion box rather than a notebook.
- Encourage students to write school-wide suggestion letters to the cafeteria, media center, principal, etc.
- Select a day of the week when student suggestions will be incorporated into the classroom.
- You can show older students the editorial section of the newspaper for real-world application.
- Show students some websites or phone numbers they can use to make comments/ suggestions on popular products.
- Model how to vary the tone of a suggestion depending on your audience.
- You may want to read the book *Armadillo Tattletale* by Helen Ketterman (Scholastic Press, 2000) to your children to explain what is appropriate.

☑ Comprehension
☑ Fluency
☐ Phonemic Awareness
☐ Phonics
☑ Vocabulary

4. Strategies for Building Fluency and Independence: Writers self-select topics and write for a variety of purposes.

Page	Mini-Lesson Topic	Literacy Center Connection	Center Title
139	Writing about what you know	Writing	"Writing Idea File"
141	Sustaining writing in literature response	Literature Response	"Write a While"
145	Using pictures as a prompt for writing	Writing	"Pick a Picture"
149	Sharing information with others to learn	Writing	"Be the Expert"

Mini-Lesson: Writing about what you know

Materials: Chart paper or overhead projector, markers
Writer's Workshop Component: Modeled Writing

1. Think aloud with your students about what you do when you don't know what to write: "Sometimes when I sit down to write, I don't know what to write about. So I think about what I know. I know about my dog, soccer, my brother, what I like to eat, and my favorite game—Clue. It helps me to keep a list of these things in my writing notebook to look at when I need writing ideas."

2. Generate a list for the students of the things you know about. Talk about how you decide what goes on the list.

3. Prior to independent writing, have students pair up and talk about what they know.

4. Together with your students, generate a list on chart paper of "Things We Can Write About."

5. Let students begin their own individual lists to be kept in their writing folder for reference.

Mini-Lesson Notes

Literacy Center Connection: Writing

Center Title: "Writing Idea File"

Have students use their "Writing Idea Files" to self-select topics for writing while they are in the Writing Center. Students select one topic from their list to write about or elaborate on. They should focus on the target skills that have been modeled during modeled- and shared-writing demonstrations. The ideas in the file can be kept on small pieces of paper and stored in the students' writing folders or on index cards attached to a key ring. Younger students can draw their lists or cut pictures from magazines to add to their idea files.

Lesson Variations and Notes

- Keep a menu of writing ideas on a chart in your Writing Center.

- Students can revisit topics they have used previously, focusing on the application of new target skills for the purposes of revision or elaboration.

- Brainstorm a list of writing genres you and your students have investigated. For example: poem, newspaper article, joke, directions, letter, fictional story, book report, etc. Add to the list as you experience new kinds of writing. Encourage students to try these out when they visit the Writing Center and during Writer's Workshop.

- Occasionally, have students share their lists with a partner or small group. As they listen to other lists, it helps them generate new ideas for their own.

☑ **Comprehension**
☑ **Fluency**
☐ **Phonemic Awareness**
☑ **Phonics**
☐ **Vocabulary**

Mini-Lesson: Sustaining writing in literature response

Materials: Selected read-aloud book, chart paper, literature response planning form (page 143), markers

Writer's Workshop Component: Shared Writing

1. Select a read-aloud text to share with the class.
2. After the reading, display a blank sheet of chart paper.
3. Think aloud about how to respond to a book: "After I read a good book, I like to share my thoughts with others who are thinking about reading the same book. I write the title of the book [record the title on the chart paper], and I write the author's name [record the author's name on the chart paper] so other readers can find this book in the library."
4. Next, write down the following statement on the chart paper: "I really liked this book!" Ask students if they think that is enough information to share with other readers. Invite them to help come up with more ideas. Discuss what makes a quality response and the importance of elaboration. Remind students that details are important when writing a response to literature. Say, "Now I need to think of some things to share about this book that will encourage others to read it. What are some things that happened in this story that we would want to share with others?"
5. Record student responses on the chart paper in list format or on an overhead transparency of the Literature Response Planning Form.

Mini-Lesson Notes

Literacy Center Connection: Literature Response

Center Title: "Write a While"

Place familiar read-aloud texts and the Literature Response Planning Forms (page 143) in a basket at your Literature Response Center. Have students complete the form in preparation for completing a written response to their reading. Place a tape player or CD player in the center so students can listen to classical music as they write their responses. Select several lengthy classical music pieces. Students can practice writing for the duration of one song to sustain their writing. Young children can draw a quality response to literature. Remind them to use details in their drawing. Students can use blank paper or the "Write a While" Response Form on page 144.

Lesson Variations and Notes

- Keep a list of reader response questions at the center to guide students' thinking.
- "Write a While" ideas could include: events in the story, character traits, students' favorite parts, interesting facts, etc.
- After students complete their writing, ask them to fill out the "Check My Writing" Self-Evaluation Form on page 148. (Note: If you notice students are not staying on topic with their writing, conduct a mini-lesson to demonstrate.)
- For students having trouble writing for the duration of the center activity, place a three-minute timer in your Writing Center. Encourage them to write until the sand runs out.
- Students also can use music to help stay on task by writing for the duration of a song.
- Students can complete the Literature Response Planning Form and a write a response after listening to a story on tape.

☑ Comprehension
☑ Fluency
☐ Phonemic Awareness
☑ Phonics
☐ Vocabulary

Literature Response Planning Form

Use this planning form to help you think of ideas before you write a literature response.

I read a (circle one):   storybook   non-fiction book   poem

Title: _____

Author: _____

I liked reading this because: _____

_____

_____

_____

_____

_____.

Ideas I might share with others are: _____

_____

_____

_____

_____

_____.

Write a While Response Form

Name: _____

My Book: _____

Use this page to draw a picture or write about your reading.

Mini-Lesson: Using pictures as a prompt for writing

Materials: A variety of photographs from magazines or calendars, chart paper, markers
Writer's Workshop Component: Shared Writing

1. Prepare a chart with a picture large enough for all students to see, and display it on an easel or board.

2. Have students sit on the floor around the easel or board.

3. Explain that you and the class are going to write about what is happening in the picture. Begin with a think-aloud: "Look at this picture of a dog. If I were writing about this picture, I might say 'This is a brown dog.' That would not be a very exciting or descriptive piece of writing. What do you notice the dog doing? What does he have in his mouth? When I write about this picture, I want to describe for the reader what he is doing. I need to choose my words carefully."

4. Encourage students to sit knee-to-knee and talk to a partner about what is happening in the picture. Ask each pair to share what they noticed with the class. (Note: Knee-to-knee conferencing and talking help promote quiet sharing.)

5. Together, write a description about the picture on the chart paper.

6. Give students other pictures to use during their independent writing time.

Mini-Lesson Notes

Literacy Center Connection: Writing

Center Title: "Pick a Picture"

Cut a variety of pictures from magazines, newspapers, advertisements, etc. Make sure the pictures are kid-friendly and full of action. Allow students to select a picture and glue or tape it to their papers. Before they begin writing, have students sit knee-to-knee with a partner and talk about what is happening in their pictures. Young children need this pre-talking to help them verbalize and plan what they will write about. Next, have students write a description about what is happening. Post the "Pick a Picture" directions from page 147 in your Writing Center to remind students what to do when they write about a picture. Additionally, you might want to keep a chart in the Writing Center to remind students to focus on writer's craft elements as they write. These can be strong verbs, color words, specific nouns, etc.

Lesson Variations and Notes

- For more information on writing about pictures, refer to Marcia Freeman's *Teaching the Youngest Writers* (Maupin House, 1998).

- While laminating pictures will allow you to reuse them, it is important for young writers to be able to keep their selected pictures with their own writing. That is why we recommend that they glue or tape the pictures to their writing.

- Another great source for pictures is an outdated calendar. The photos are clear and cover a variety of topics.

- Younger writers might only write one or two words in the beginning. As they become more proficient, the quantity and quality will increase.

- Allow students to sit knee-to-knee to share their writing during other writing lessons.

- For documenting the growth of your writers, consider using picture-prompted writing multiple times during the year. Having students write about the same picture each time allows you to see growth in writing by eliminating the variable of topic selection.

- Students can use the "Check My Writing" self-evaluation form on page 148.

☑ **Comprehension**
☑ **Fluency**
☐ **Phonemic Awareness**
☑ **Phonics**
☑ **Vocabulary**

Pick a Picture

1. Choose a picture.

2. Think about what is happening in the picture.

3. Write down some words or draw a picture to help show what the picture makes you think about.

4. Write about your picture.

5. Read your writing to a friend.

Checking My Writing	Checking My Writing
Name: _____	**Name:** _____

Is my writing on topic at the beginning?

☺ Yes 😐 I don't know ☹ No

Is my writing on topic in the middle?

☺ Yes 😐 I don't know ☹ No

Is my writing on topic at the end?

☺ Yes 😐 I don't know ☹ No

Did I need more time?

☺ Yes 😐 I don't know ☹ No

Is my writing on topic at the beginning?

☺ Yes 😐 I don't know ☹ No

Is my writing on topic in the middle?

☺ Yes 😐 I don't know ☹ No

Is my writing on topic at the end?

☺ Yes 😐 I don't know ☹ No

Did I need more time?

☺ Yes 😐 I don't know ☹ No

Mini-Lesson: Sharing information with others to learn

Materials: Transparency or chart paper, *Yellow Pages* from a phonebook, "Be the Expert" Planning Form (page 151)

Writer's Workshop Component: Modeled Writing

1. Bring in photos, books, and/or objects related to a topic you know a lot about and feel comfortable sharing.

2. Begin with a think-aloud: "I love to write, especially when I am writing about something that I know a lot about. I love to scrapbook. In fact, I scrapbook so much that I have become an expert. Let me show you how I learned about scrapbooking."

3. Share idea books and real examples with the students. Continue thinking aloud: "Now I want to share with others what I know in case they want to learn about scrapbooking, too."

4. Model filling out the "Be the Expert" Planning Form on the overhead.

5. Note: This lesson may take more than one day. Simply return to the plan the next day and begin writing about the topic.

6. Show students the *Yellow Pages* from your local phonebook. Explain how people use these as a resource to find an expert. Tell students that as they publish their writing, you will create a class book called "Find an Expert." This will help them learn how to access information about what their classmates know when they want to learn something new.

Mini-Lesson Notes

Literacy Center Connection: Writing

Center Title: "Be the Expert"

Have students refer to their "Writing Idea Files" in their writer's notebook (see page 140). Have students select one topic they feel they are experts on. Place copies of the "Be the Expert" Planning Form (page 151) at the center. After students complete the plan, have them write as much as they can about the topic. This could take several days. Publish the students' writing in a class book titled "Find an Expert." This class book can be used as a resource by the students in the room when they need to do research or want to learn about a topic.

Lesson Variations and Notes

- Create different expert books by designating a specific topic such as sports, animals, hobbies, food, etc.

- Have adults record the students' writing on tape. Place a tape player at the Writing Center for students to listen to and learn about topics that interest them.

- Younger students can draw what they are experts about and dictate their stories.

- Have students write to experts in the community to learn about new topics.

- Make a list of "Expert Ideas" and keep it posted at the Writing Center. Write "I am an expert about…" at the top, and include topics such as authors, books, math, science, games, cars, dinosaurs, bugs, countries, etc.

☑ **Comprehension**
☑ **Fluency**
☐ **Phonemic Awareness**
☑ **Phonics**
☑ **Vocabulary**

Be the Expert

Expert's name: _____

I know a lot about: _____.

I know about this topic because (check all that apply):

____ I have read books about it.

____ I have tried it.

____ I have seen it on T.V.

____ Someone taught me about it.

Important words about my topic: _____

_____

_____

_____

_____

_____

_____

_____

_____.

Teacher Resources

Library

Research Center

Writing Center

My Poems

Poetry Center

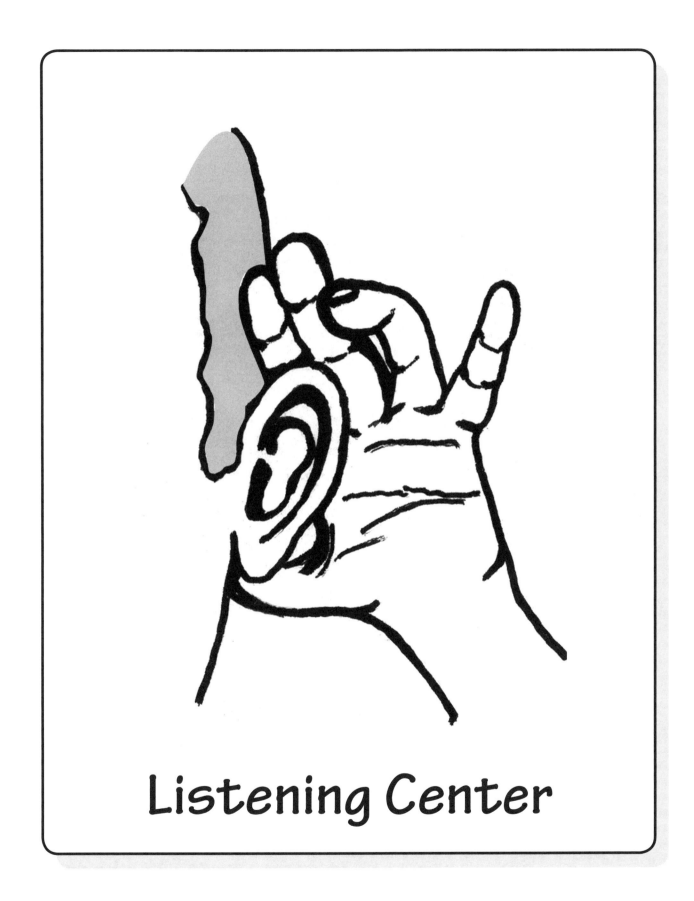

Listening Center

Word Work Center

A Quick-Start Guide to Literacy Centers

Walk down any elementary school classroom during the first few weeks of school and you will hear, "We keep the ____ here," "Only use small dabs of glue," "Remember to put books back on the shelves neatly," or "We *walk* in our classroom." Teachers are preparing their students to function in the classroom environment and be able to work independently. In *The First Days of School* (Harry K. Wong Publications, Inc., 2001), classroom management consultant Harry Wong writes, "Student achievement at the end of the year is directly related to the degree to which the teacher establishes good control of the classroom procedures in the very first week of the school year." A well-designed classroom helps everyone function better. When you plan for the physical space in your classroom, you must plan how you will familiarize students with acceptable movement, noise level, and use of materials. Many teachers want to rush the process of set-up. Don't. Take time and model the use of centers as well as the use of materials within them. No matter when during the school year you read this book, you can make your learning environment optimal for you and your students by thinking carefully about your physical environment, management of materials, and student responsibility during center time.

A List of Possible Literacy Centers and Their Purposes

Although many different centers can be set up in the elementary classroom, we recommend setting up seven literacy centers first. The centers we describe in *More Primary Literacy Centers* will regenerate themselves throughout the year when you stock them with materials which encourage open-ended activities and allow student choice within them. As you plan your objectives and expectations for each literacy center, consider some of the supplies suggested in the "Have It/Want It" charts beginning on page 169 to encourage student-generated responses to reading and writing. These centers allow integration of content-area materials and open-ended responses, as well as oral and written manipulation of language. See the following table listing all of the centers, along with their purposes.

Name of Center	Purpose
Classroom Library	Provides students with a variety of print and genre to practice reading skills and strategies
Listening	Increases speaking, reading, and writing vocabulary; allows students to self-monitor fluency and progress in reading
Literature Response	Gives students the opportunity to authentically respond to a text they have read or heard
Poetry	Encourages students to read and perform various poems with fluency and expression; exposes the struggling reading to rhyme, rhythm, and repetition
Research	Integrates the study of science and social studies into the literacy hour; provides children time to interact with non-fiction text
Spelling/Word Work	Allows students to manipulate letters and words which can be integrated into their reading and writing experiences
Writing	Provides opportunity for children to practice the writer's craft and target skills through self-selected topics and methods of presentation

Additional Centers

You may want to add other centers for your students during the literacy block. Many early childhood classrooms have centers such as art, blocks, housekeeping, dramatic play, and math. If you are currently using any or all of these centers, as you read this book consider ways to bump up the level of literacy taking place within them.

For example, you may want to add cookbooks, newspapers, phone books, and notepads to housekeeping to simulate ways literacy is used in the home. Your block center may become a car repair shop where children write bills, read magazines, and give estimates for work. There are many other ideas you will think of for adding literacy to traditional centers. After you decide how you will do this, consider which of the aforementioned literacy centers you would like to add to your classroom. A clear picture of what you want will help you as you continue to read this book.

Physical Environment

Decide which centers you will establish in your classroom and then plan for your physical environment. While there are many options for setting up a classroom, we suggest separating the noisier areas from those which require quiet more focused work. The centers where talking is important, such as writing, poetry, and research, should be together to promote collaboration among students. Centers such as classroom library, listening, and literature response more often require participants to focus on their individual work and should be placed in areas of the room where quiet is respected. This will help minimize distractions for students as they complete their work.

Consider where you plan to conduct small group work while students are engaged in centers. Position yourself so you can conduct the small group effectively while monitoring student participation in centers. See pages 167 and 168 for two samples of primary classroom maps.

From Mellissa: *In the back of my classroom, I set up three small tables in a U-shape. This makes a cozy nook for small group work. The students sit facing me to keep them focused on the small group lesson. Positioning myself in the center allows me to interact with all of the students in the small group, as well as monitor the rest of my classroom center activities.*

Acquiring Materials

A well-stocked center will be a busy and inviting place for students. The "Have It/Want It" charts on pages 169-175 are designed to help you start thinking about materials you might want to include in your centers.

Student Responsibility

While a well-stocked center can be highly engaging, it can also break down when materials are misused, limited, or unfamiliar. Students must be taught to take responsibility for their learning environment before they can be expected to learn independently. Involving them in the process of set-up will help build a sense of ownership and community in your classroom. Teaching procedures for material use before opening any center for independent work will lead to a more successful learning experience for you and your students.

From Susan: *My first-graders spent weeks learning how to click marker caps back on so they wouldn't dry out. I modeled it and we practiced together. I can still picture them sitting on the floor with markers right by their ears listening for the click. When they finally learned how, I let them use markers in centers.*

Christine Saunders teaches her kindergarten students this little rhyme: "If you don't hear it click, the marker will get sick!" Christine's students know that taking care of classroom supplies is everyone's responsibility. They understand that careful handling and use of materials allow them to continue to be able to use them during their center time. This type of modeling and practice is critical for student success in the center-oriented classroom.

Kids must know what is expected of them while they are in each center, from simple tasks such as stapling papers together to how to clean up when they are finished. Demonstration is only the beginning of showing them what you want to happen during the work time. They must also practice the procedure with you. When you give them practice time, it allows you to see their level of understanding and make any changes necessary.

Carolyn Kelly sets up centers with her first-grade students in a class meeting. At the beginning of the year, they sit together in an area she has designated for the center. Together they make a "Looks Like/Sounds Like" chart. She asks them to think about the center, the type of work that will go on there, and the way it will look and sound when being used properly. The students help generate a list of what the center should look like and sound like when in use.

Research Center	
Looks Like:	**Sounds Like:**
• Kids using tools carefully • Recording our research • Thinking about what we learn	• Talking softly to a partner about our work • Materials being moved around quietly • Quiet voices

Carolyn keeps the chart posted in the center. During the year, she and her students refer to it and revise it to keep the center running smoothly. This repeated practice helps Carolyn's students know and understand her expectations of the learning environment.

When students demonstrate an understanding of the expectations within a center, you have the right and responsibility to let them know when it breaks down and to make changes as necessary. Occasionally, make a list of all of those things that make you think your classroom is not running smoothly or that impede your students' learning process. Is it the student who uses forty-seven staples to put her book together? Is it the glue bottles left out with glue drying around them? Is it paper not stacked neatly when it is returned? Perhaps it's the student who is constantly tugging at your pants leg and asking, "What do I do now?" Have a class meeting to demonstrate and model what you expect your students to do during independent work time. You can expect to hold several class meetings throughout the year as problems arise.

Use some of your class meetings to talk about what would help your students function better in class. Let them share problems and suggest solutions at the class meeting. This helps them see that you are all a part of a learning community. It builds responsibility and begins to help them understand the flexibility in the classroom environment. Most importantly, you are preparing your students to work independently while you teach small groups.

Teacher Tips for Successful Set-Up
Following is a list of ideas for successful set-up of literacy centers. These ideas have been collected from many of our colleagues based on their classroom experiences.

- **Clearly label supply bins and shelves.** Young children may need pictures or drawings of items that belong in each storage bin. Use a black marker and tagboard to make clear labels. Attach these labels to your bins and shelves using clear packaging tape. Students will be able to look around your room and see very clearly where you expect items to be put away after use.

- **Establish clear boundaries for your centers.** Your students must be able to understand where each center begins and ends. Use your classroom furniture, rugs, hula hoops, or appliance boxes to section off spaces for each center. Place a label or icon in the center so your students will be able to identify it. When you decide where each center will be, sit in the chair you will use in your small group space and be sure you have clear visual access to student activity.

- **Open one center at a time.** When you are first beginning centers, only open one at a time until you know that your students understand the routines and procedures required for proper use. Allow children to rotate to and from the center in a shortened center time, or "trial time." Be sure to discuss as a class what goes well and what needs improvement. Add to or change your "Looks Like/Sounds Like" charts.

- **Create a center management chart/rotation.** Several center management charts are explained on page 165. Help your students understand your system in the beginning so they know exactly where they should be during literacy center time.

- **Minimize teacher interruptions.** Mellissa designates center captains in her room. She selects students who know and understand what should be happening within each center. Each of these students wears a clothespin during center time. Other classmates know when they have a question they must go ask the center captain. If the captain is unable to answer the question, he may go ask Mellissa. Since this is the only person allowed "teacher access" during small groups, it minimizes distractions from other students.

- **Determine a signal for clean-up time.** It is hard for young children to just stop what they are doing. Help them prepare to stop by giving a five-minute warning. Many teachers use a bell or sing a song when it is time to clean up centers. Whatever signal you choose, use it consistently so your children understand that they must stop what they are doing and clean up.

Maximizing Space

Space for centers is limited in some classrooms. While some centers may be at designated tables, shelves, or corners around the perimeter of the classroom, others may be stored in plastic tubs or bags which are placed on student desks during literacy center time. Here are some suggestions to help you maximize your space:

- **Gift Bags.** Store centers in gift bags. Students can bring the bag to their seat during literacy center time. The teacher fills the bag with books related to the pictures on the outside. For example, a fish bag would be filled with fiction and non-fiction books about the ocean, ocean word cards to alphabetize, fish stamps and stickers to write about the ocean, and poetry cards with fish pointers for fluency building.

- **Children's Lunch Boxes.** You can store center activities and supplies in children's lunch boxes. These can often be found at garage sales at very low cost.

- **Cereal Boxes.** Collect empty cereal boxes from your students. Cut the box as shown in the diagram. Use these boxes to store small books, magazines, and small pointers for book browsing.

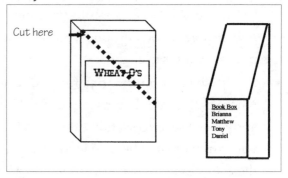

- **Miniature Garbage Cans.** Miniature garbage cans can be found at the dollar store. You can also use one-gallon ice cream buckets for cans. Place these in each center for students to throw away their small scraps. Make emptying the trash part of your daily center clean-up. This will minimize the movement across your classroom to discard trash and keep your centers tidy.

- **Shoe Boxes.** Shoe boxes, either cardboard or plastic, make great center containers. They can be moved to a student desk or floor space for students to work during literacy center time.

- **Clothesline.** Attach a clothesline under your chalk tray. Store centers in plastic storage bags and clip them to the line. When students are ready to work in centers, they can go get a bag and take it to a designated work area.

- **Hula Hoops.** Hula Hoops spread out on the floor make nice center work spaces. Children know exactly where the boundaries are, and the materials stay in one place.

Managing Centers

Many teachers start centers without a clear management system. Don't. If you want centers to run smoothly, good management is critical. Decide on important questions regarding your literacy centers before you start. Should students visit each center daily? Weekly? Bi-weekly? How will you monitor your students' use of centers? How do you want children to move during the literacy center time?

A clear, understandable center organization will help your students know exactly what you expect. Following you will find some ideas for managing student movement during center time. Try one or two to find the one that's right for you. You will have to model how to read and interpret the chart you choose many times with your students. Once they understand, it will help you pull together small groups without worrying whether or not they are following your directions.

We have provided center icons for you on pages 153-158 in the Teacher Resources. These can be used to create any of the center management systems that follow.

Management Board. Cluster your centers into groups of two or three. Below each cluster, place a list of five or six children. Rotate the lists each day to a new cluster of centers. Place your chart at the children's eye level and in a place where they can refer to it as they move through their assigned centers.

Pocket Chart. Use the pocket chart much the same way you would the management board. Write each student's name on an index card. Group students next to the center or centers they should complete that day. You will need to provide some options in case students finish their work in their assigned center before center time has ended. Some options might include reading a book, writing a letter, reading or writing in their journals, reading the room, using the listening center, etc.

Second-grade teacher *Cathy Corona* puts a bright-colored index card behind one student's name for each center on her pocket chart. This is the designated center captain who is responsible for seeing that the materials are being used properly. The captain also checks to see that the center is cleaned up at the end of center time.

Center Contract. Provide each student with a contract. As they work in a center, they record their progress on their contract. Some teachers like to follow this up with a daily learning log where students write what they did during center time and their plans for next time. (See pages 176 and 177 for samples.)

Work Wheel. This system works like the management board. Place center icons on a large, cardboard pizza wheel divided into four sections. Write each student's name on a clothespin. Each day, attach the clothespin to the wheel showing where each child should work. Rotate the clothespins daily.

Use this information and the space below to design your own center management system.

Name of Center	# of students	Location in room	Quiet or talking?	How often will they visit?	Product or process?	Do I have materials?

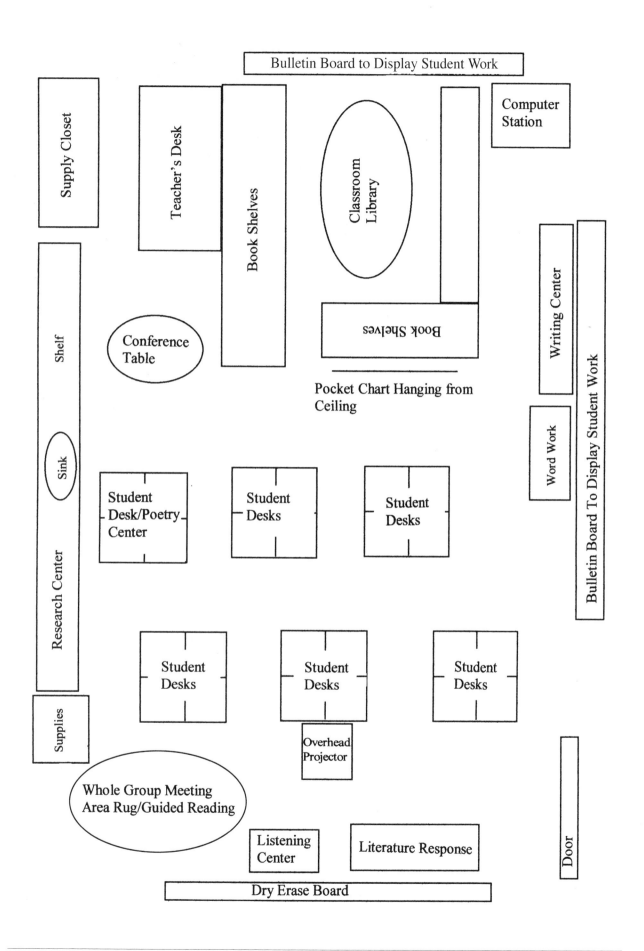

Bulletin Board to Display Student Work

Supply Closet

Teacher's Desk

Book Shelves

Classroom Library

Computer Station

Shelf

Conference Table

Book Shelves

Pocket Chart Hanging from Ceiling

Writing Center

Word Work

Bulletin Board To Display Student Work

Sink

Research Center

Student Desk/Poetry Center

Student Desks

Student Desks

Supplies

Student Desks

Student Desks

Student Desks

Overhead Projector

Whole Group Meeting Area Rug/Guided Reading

Listening Center

Literature Response

Door

Dry Erase Board

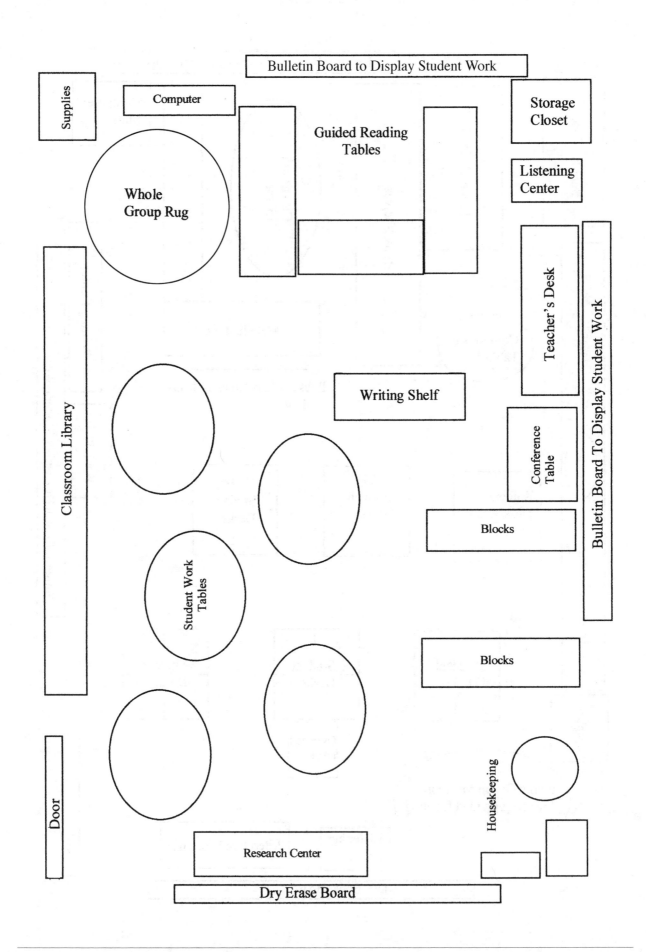

Classroom Library

Have It	Want It	Material Name	Description/Notes
		books	The classroom library should be stocked with fiction and non-fiction books at a variety of reading levels.
		class-made books	Honor student work by placing class-produced books in your library.
		magazines	Keep a bin of magazines for kids. After they have read these, they can cut out the pictures to place in the writing center.
		newspapers	Check with your local paper to see about their Newspapers in Education program.
		comfortable pillows or chairs	Place bean bags, large pillows, or child-sized chairs in your library to provide a comfortable place to read.
		bins for storage	Organize your books by author, topic, illustrator, etc. Label for easy student accessibility.
		shelves	When possible, turn some books so that the covers are displayed rather than the spines.
		labels for bins and shelves	Labels can be made by author, genre, or difficulty of book. Use colored dots on the labels and place the corresponding colored dot on the book spine for easy reorganization.
		class-generated writing charts	Students love to re-read their own writing. Keep these charts at eye level for students to revisit in your library.
		reading glasses	Use old sunglasses with the lenses popped out. Students love to wear glasses when they read.
		pointers	Keep a bucket of pointers handy for students as they reread charts, big books, poems, etc.
		lamps	Lamps add a cozy touch to a reading corner.
		carpet	Carpet squares or a large area rug add comfortable boundaries to the library space.

Listening Center

Have It	Want It	Material Name	Description/Notes
		books or poems on tape	Many publishers produce tapes to accompany their books.
		baskets or plastic bins to organize book selections	Place the book and audiotape in a gallon-size resealable bag. Label each piece with a colored dot for easy clean-up.
		cassette player	Label the buttons on your cassette player as follows: green dot = play, red dot = stop. Mark the volume dial with a line of white-out to keep the volume under control.
		blank audio cassettes	Use these for students to record their own reading. Place in the student portfolio for assessment and evaluation. Parents can listen to this tape during conferences with you.
		Language Master	Purchase pre-recorded cards or record your own.
		paper for response	Add writing to the listening center by having students write a response to a book (i.e., draw or write a retelling, tell your favorite part, write what you learned, etc.).
		pencils, pens, markers, crayons	Cover and label empty juice cans for storage. Keep a can of sharpened pencils available for students to trade in broken ones.
		baby wipes	Keep disposable baby cloths on hand to clean earphones after use.
		film strip view	Many media centers have old individual film strip viewers. Use these for students to listen and view at this center.
		individual cassette players	Students can use these instead of the larger listening center.
		listening log	Have students keep a reading log posted at the reading center of books they have heard.

Literature Response Center

Have It	Want It	Material Name	Description/Notes
		books	Use familiar shared or guided reading text for students to revisit as they respond.
		magazines	Students can locate an interesting picture or article and write a response. Older readers may want to submit an editorial to the magazine.
		literature response matrix	See page 27. Students choose a response idea from the matrix to complete after reading.
		paper	Supply paper in a variety of sizes and colors to encourage creative response.
		scissors, glue, tape, stapler	Discount stores often have inexpensive tubs which can be used to organize these items.
		schema connection chart	Students make connections between what they read and what they know.
		journals	Students respond to reading through their writing. They can dialogue with another student, write to a character, tell a favorite part, etc.
		markers, crayons, pencils, pens	Organize into cans or bins for easy access.
		sticky notes	As students revisit text, they can add sticky notes to pages which make them think, fell, or remember something.
		inquiry questions	Post question stems for students to use in their response journals.
		critic review board	Have students write a critique of a book or article they have read. Post these in the response center.

Poetry Center

Have It	Want It	Material Name	Description/Notes
		books of poems	Label by author, topics, anthologies, etc.
		poetry charts	Purchase from educational suppliers or create your own on chart paper.
		interactive file folder poems	Convert interactive chart poems to smaller file folders for individual student use.
		computer-generated poems	Use your desktop publisher to illustrate poetry from shared and guided reading.
		pocket chart	Write poems on sentence strips and place in a pocket chart for students to order and innovate.
		overhead projector	Copy familiar poems onto overhead transparencies. Students can use pointers and overhead pens to read, illustrate, or innovate poems. Store these poems in a three-ring binder near your overhead projector.
		pointers	Keep a can of small and large pointers for students to track print in this center.
		class poetry notebook	As you read poems together, compile a notebook of favorites for students to review throughout the year.
		magnetic poetry word cards	Purchase or create your own magnetic poetry words. Students can use these words to compose their own poems.
		individual poetry notebooks	Copy familiar poems on small sheets of paper. Students choose one poem each week to insert and illustrate in their own poetry notebook. Have students use tape or a glue stick to attach their poems. This keeps the pages from sticking together.
		pens, pencils, highlighters	Students can revisit poems in their notebooks and highlight rhyming words, strong verbs, word patterns, etc.
		tape	Use to affix poems inside notebooks.
		scissors	Use your storage can to display beautiful language you have read or words you want your students to remember.

Research Center

Have It	Want It	Material Name	Description/Notes
		non-fiction books	Keep books clearly labeled and organized by theme, topic, or author in bins or baskets.
		maps	Get laminated maps from your local insurance agent.
		attraction/travel brochures	Use brochures found in local hotels, restaurants, and travel agencies.
		sorting bin	A kitchen relish tray with several compartments works well for this. Students can sort and classify different items related to topic of study.
		magnifying glasses, a balance, rulers, and tweezers	Keep these items available for students to use when observing, classifying, and sorting items in the Research Center.
		properties chart	List attributes (colors, size, shape, weight, etc.) on a chart (see page 120). Have students describe the object in an observation log.
		pens, pencils, markers, and highlighters	Students need a variety of writing utensils to record their observations in the center.
		inquiry chart	Write several question stems on a chart. Students can use this chart as they record their thinking and observations at this center.
		empty food boxes	Create question cards to accompany familiar food boxes.
		observation sheets	Students can use a clipboard and glasses as they record their observations and investigations at this center.
		thematic vocabulary charts or word rings	Keep specialized or thematic vocabulary organized on charts, in a file folder, or on index cards bound with a ring. (Label with stickers, photos, or pictures for younger students.)
		non-fiction magazines and newspapers	Provide a basket of children's magazines and newspapers to promote independent study of high-interest topics.
		clipboards	Use with observation sheets and other scientific investigations.

Spelling/Word Work Center

Have It	Want It	Material Name	Description/Notes
		letter tiles	These can be made using one-inch square ceramic tiles from the home improvement store. Write a letter on each tile using permanent marker. Use blue for consonants and red for vowels. Protect them using clear nail polish.
		plastic or foam letters	Use these for sorting, making words, and student exploration.
		magnetic letters	Aluminum cookie sheets work well for practicing using letters and words. Letters can also be stored in cookie tins. The lids of the tins double as a work board.
		dry erase boards and markers	Students can write and notice word patterns and sounds within words. Purchase kitchen backsplash at your local home improvement center and have it cut to 12" x 18".
		word cards	Use the pictures from old workbooks, worksheets, or magazines to make illustrated word cards for students to sort.
		rubber letter stamps	Students can use the letter stamps to make word family lists, reproduce spelling lists, and/or work with word patterns.
		magic slates, Magna Doodles®	Use these to practice letter formation, word patterns, spelling, etc.
		letter sorting cans	Margarine tubs or juice cans labeled with letters or word patterns can be used for sorting small toys and trinkets.
		paper, sticky notes, writing tools	Keep plenty of these supplies on hand to encourage students to try out new words, patterns, or sounds.
		Wikki Stix®, pipe cleaners, play dough/ clay	Students can use these to form letters and words. Wikki Stix® can be stored on vinyl placemats.
		alphabet macaroni or cereal	Students can glue these onto index cards to make words and sentences.
		newspapers, dictionary, thesaurus	Students must know how to use reference materials to locate and explore unknown words and meanings.

Writing Center

Have It	Want It	Material Name	Description/Notes
		variety of paper	Provide a wide variety of shapes, colors, and sizes to maintain student interest while working in the center.
		blank books	Use wallpaper samples books for covers. Staple 4-6 sheets of paper folded in half inside the covers.
		writing tools	Provide a variety of pens, pencils, crayons, and markers for student writing.
		staplers	Model how to use one or two staples to attach papers.
		hole punch, paper clips, tape, highlighters	Students can use these supplies to create small books, edit, or organize materials
		dry erase white boards	Purchase kitchen backsplash at the home improvement center and have it cut to 12" x 18".
		rubber stamps, pads, and stickers	Picture stamps, stickers, and letter stamps can help children with illustrating and composing.
		envelopes	Ask greeting card companies/stores and print shops to donate envelopes to your classroom.
		clipboards	Clipboards free students to work in comfortable corners of the room.
		writing idea file and/ or picture file	Keep a list of topics to write about for students to reference. The picture file is a springboard for student writing ideas.
		mini-dictionaries	These can be made from stickers, worksheets, computer icons, etc.
		dictionary/thesaurus	Make sure these are age-appropriate and user-friendly.
		word wall	Word walls should be displayed for easy physical access during writing.
		computer	Use this for publishing student writing.
		thematic vocabulary chart	Use stickers, old worksheets, or magazines to make a chart of thematic vocabulary. Keep this posted during the entire unit to encourage use of these words in writing.

My Name: _____

Daily Learning Log

Center Name	Mon.	Tues.	Wed.	Thurs.	Fri.
Classroom Library					
Listening					
Literature Response					
Poetry					
Research					
Word Work					
Writing					
My free choice this week: _____					

("A Quick-Start Guide to Literacy Centers," ©2001 Alonso & Nations, *Primary Literacy Centers: Making Reading and Writing STICK!*)

_____'s Independent Learning Log

Date	Name of Center	What I did today...	Evidence of my learning—a product, a friend's initials, etc.	Reflections on my learning: How can this help me in other areas?

("A Quick-Start Guide to Literacy Centers," ©2001 Alonso & Nations, *Primary Literacy Centers: Making Reading and Writing STICK!*)

Center Contract

My Name:_____	My Name:_____
Week of:_____	Week of:_____
The centers I did this week are:	The centers I did this week are:
What I learned is:	What I learned is:

My work this week

Name:_____

Color each shape when you finish the center

Classroom
Library

Listening

Word Work

Research

Writing

Poetry

Center Learning Reflection Log

Name: _____ Date: _____

These are the center(s) I completed today:

☐ _____   ☐ _____

☐ _____   ☐ _____

☐ _____   ☐ _____

☐ _____   ☐ _____

This is what I learned or practiced:

This is how I feel about my learning:

☺   😐   ☹

My plan for tomorrow:

"Looks Like/Sounds Like" Chart

👁 Looks Like	👂 Sounds Like

Student Interview

1. **How often do you read books?**
   - ○ Every day
   - ○ Most days
   - ○ Not often

2. **What is your favorite thing to read about?**

   _____

   _____

   _____

3. **What is your favorite center in our classroom? Why?**

   _____

   _____

   _____

   _____

4. **If you could learn anything at all this year, what would it be?**

   _____

   _____

   _____

5. **What is your favorite thing about school? Explain why.**

   _____

   _____

   _____

   _____

6. **What is your least favorite thing about school? Explain why.**

   _____

   _____

   _____

Center Evaluation Form

Center name:

Number of students participating in this center at one time: _____

Current activities available in this center:

When I watched students in this center, I noticed:

Things I need to address:

Activities/materials to add:

Student Work/Observation Form

Student name: _____   Date: _____

Center(s) the student was observed in:

Student activities during observation:

On-task behavior rubric:

1—Mostly on-task with very few distractions

2—Student occasionally spends time off-task without disrupting others

3—Student occasionally spends time off-task and disrupts others

4—Student off-task for duration of observation (required re-direction)

Interaction with others:

1—Student works well with others

2—Student works primarily alone

3—Student disrupts other students' learning

4—Student does not interact well with others

Notes for follow-up mini-lessons with this student:

Student Work/Observation Form

Student name: _____   Date: _____

Center(s) the student was observed in:

Student activities during observation:

On-task behavior rubric:

1—Mostly on-task with very few distractions

2—Student occasionally spends time off-task without disrupting others

3—Student occasionally spends time off-task and disrupts others

4—Student off-task for duration of observation (required re-direction)

Interaction with others:

1—Student works well with others

2—Student works primarily alone

3—Student disrupts other students' learning

4—Student does not interact well with others

Notes for follow-up mini-lessons with this student:

14 Ways to Use a Playback Pipe

- **Segment and blend words with it.** The playback pipe is often referred to as a "phonics phone." This tool helps you hear phonemes in words. Break apart words ("cat=c-a-t") as well as put them back together orally ("d-o-g=dog").
- **Practice sentences.** Find some sentences with a variety of punctuation. Practice reading the sentence with the right "voice" for the punctuation mark.
- **Read poetry.** Maya Angelou says that poetry is meant to be read aloud. Read orally and listen to the language of a poem using the playback pipe.
- **Read a book.** Practice reading a book in it.
- **Give characters a voice.** Use the playback pipe to help you read the voices of the characters to make a story more meaningful.
- **Interview a friend.** Write some questions that you would like to ask a friend. Use the playback pipe as your interview phone.
- **Edit your writing.** Stop occasionally during your writing to read it into the playback pipe. This will help you edit your own work.
- **Edit someone else's writing.** Use the playback pipe to read someone else's writing.
- **Housekeeping phone.** Use the playback pipe as a phone. Provide more than one to encourage authentic conversation.
- **Read a book to a stuffed animal.** Children love an audience for their reading. Let them read to a stuffed animal using the playback pipe. This will help improve their fluency.
- **Read the room.** Use it to read the room. This will help control noise level as readers move throughout the room practicing their fluency.
- **Perform a poem or short story.** Practice a poem or short story for performance. Read it several times into the playback pipe to get the right voice inflections.
- **Practice your spelling words.** Use the playback pipe to say your words and then spell them.
- **Practice your math facts.** Use the playback pipe to practice your math facts.

My Name: _____

My Weekly Buddy Reading Record

Date	Who listened to you?	What did you read?	What did you think about your reading?

* Store this form in your Homework Folder and turn it in every Friday morning.

Try-It-Out Log

Try the word	Look in our room and try again	A friend's try	My teacher's turn	I write it the right way

Literacy Response Chart with Explanations

Wow Sheet

See page 116 for the Literacy Connection Planner that explains this response.

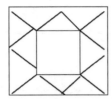

Character Frame

Have students fold the paper into a square as shown. Make the frame opening in the middle of the paper. Have students draw a picture of the character in the middle of the frame. They can write interesting things the character in their book says or does under each flap.

Create a Caption

Have students use a picture from their book and create a caption on a sticky note or index card. You can lay a photo with its caption on the copy machine to display these in your Research Center.

Write an Ending

Students can write a new ending for a story or article that they have read.

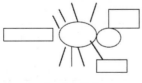

Label It

Have students draw an animal or plant from an informational text they have read and label its parts.

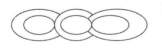

Make a Connection

Students should write or draw a text-to-text or text-to-self connection they can make with a character or event in their story. Remind them to tell how this connection helps them understand the story better.

Literacy Connection Planner

Mini-Lesson:

Materials:

Reader's Workshop Component:

Mini-Lesson Notes

Literacy Center Connection:

Center Title:

Lesson Variation and Notes:

Literacy Connection Planner

Mini-Lesson:

Materials:

Writer's Workshop Component:

Mini-Lesson Notes

Literacy Center Connection:

Center Title:

Lesson Variation and Notes:

A Quick Reference Guide to Center Activities

Professional References and Resources

Allington, Richard L. *What Really Matters for Struggling Readers: Designing Research-Based Programs.* Boston, MA: Allyn & Bacon, 2000.

Clay, Marie M. *An Observation Survey of Early Literacy Achievement.* Portsmouth, NH: Heinemann, 1993.

_____. *Reading Recovery: A Guidebook for Teachers in Training.* Portsmouth, NH: Heinemann, 1993.

Cunningham, Patricia M., and Richard L. Allington. *Classrooms That Work: They Can All Read and Write* (2nd ed.). Reading, MA: Addison-Wesley Longman, 1999.

_____. and Dorothy P. Hall. *Making Words.* Carthage, IL: Good Apple, 1994.

Dorn, L. J., French, C., & Jones, T. *Apprenticeship in Literacy: Transitions across Reading and Writing.* York, ME: Stenhouse Publishers, 1998.

_____. and Carla Soffos. *Shaping Literate Minds.* Portland, ME: Stenhouse, 2001.

Dudley-Marling, Curt and Patricia Paugh. *A Classroom Teacher's Guide to Struggling Readers.* Portsmouth, NH: Heinemann, 2004.

Fisher, Bobbi. *Thinking and Learning Together: Curriculum and Community in a Primary Classroom.* Portsmouth, NH: Heinemann, 1995.

Fountas, Irene C. and Gay S. Pinnell. *Guided Reading: Good First Teaching for All Children.* Portsmouth NH: Heinemann, 1996.

Graves, Donald H. *The Energy to Teach.* Portsmouth, NH: Heinemann, 2001.

Harp, Bill. *The Handbook of Literacy Assessment and Evaluation.* Norwood, MA: Christopher-Gordon Publishers, 1996.

Harvey, Stephanie and Goudvis, Anne. *Strategies That Work: Teaching Comprehension to Enhance Understanding.* Portland, ME: Stenhouse, 2000.

Hiebert, E. H., Pearson, P. D., Taylor, B. M., Richardson, V., & Paris, S. G. *Every Child a Reader: Applying Reading Research in the Classroom.* Ann Arbor, MI: Center for the Improvement of Early Reading Achievement, 1998.

Holdaway, Don. *The Foundations of Literacy.* Sydney: Ashton Scholastic, distributed by Heinemann, Portsmouth, NH, 1997.

Jacobs, Heidi Hayes. *Getting Results with Curriculum Mapping.* Alexandria, VA: Association for Supervision and Curriculum Development, 2004.

Jacobs, Heidi Hayes. *Mapping the Big Picture: Integrating Curriculum & Assessment K-12.* Alexandria, VA: Association for Supervision and Curriculum Development, 1997.

Keene, Ellin Oliver and Susan Zimmermann. *Mosaic of Thought: Teaching Comprehension in a Reader's Workshop.* Portsmouth, NH: Heinemann, 1997.

Miller, Debbie. *Reading with Meaning: Teaching Comprehension in the Primary Grades.* Portland, ME: Stenhouse, 2002.

Mooney, Margaret E. *Reading to, with, and by Children.* Katonah, NY: Richard C. Owen, 1990.

National Reading Panel. *Teaching Children to Read: An Evidence-Based Assessment of the Scientific Research Literature on Reading and Its Implications for Reading Instruction.* Washington D.C.: National Institute of Child Health and Human Development, 2000.

Nations, Susan and Mellissa Alonso. *Primary Literacy Centers: Making Reading and Writing STICK!* Gainesville, FL: Maupin House, 2001.

Nations, Susan and Suzi Boyett. *So Much Stuff, So Little Space: Creating and Managing the Learner-Centered Classroom.* Gainesville, FL: Maupin House, 2002.

Parkes, Brenda. *Read It Again! Revisiting Shared Reading,* Portsmouth, NH: Stenhouse, 2000.

Payne, Ruby K. *A Framework for Understanding Poverty.* Highlands, TX: aha! Process, Inc., 2001.

Pearson, P. David, and M.C. Gallagher. "The Instruction of Reading Comprehension." *Contemporary Educational Psychology* 8:317 – 344. 1983.

Pearson, P., Dole, J., Duffy, G., and Roehler, L. "Developing Expertise in Reading Comprehension: What Should Be Taught and How Should It Be Taught?" In *What Research Has to Say to the Teacher of Reading (2nd ed.),* edited by J. Farstup and S.M. Samuels. Newark, DE: International Reading Association, 1992.

Rasinski, Timothy and Nancy Padak. *Effective Reading Strategies: Teaching Children Who Find Reading Difficult.* Upper Saddle River, NJ: Pearson Education, 2004.

_____. *The Fluent Reader: Oral Reading Strategies for Building Word Recognition, Fluency, and Comprehension.* Jefferson City, MO: Scholastic, 2003.

Routman, Regie. *Conversations: Strategies for Teaching, Learning, and Evaluating.* Portsmouth, NH: Heinemann, 2000.

_____. *Reading Essentials: The Specifics You Need to Teach Reading Well.* Portsmouth, NH: Heinemann, 2003.

Snow, Catherine E., M. Susan Burns, and Peg Griffin, editors. *Preventing Reading Difficulties in Young Children.* Washington, D.C.: National Academies Press, 1998.

Tomlinson, Carol Ann. *The Differentiated Classroom: Responding to the Needs of All Learners.* Alexandria, VA: Association for Supervision and Curriculum Development, 1999.

U.S. Department of Education. *Part B – Student Reading Skills Improvement Grants* [online]. U.S. Department of Education, 2004. Available from World Wide Web: http://www.ed.gov/policy/elsec/leg/esea02/pg4.html

Yatvin, Joanne. *A Room with a Differentiated View.* Portsmouth, NH: Heinemann, 2004.

List of Cited Children's Literature

Berger, Melvin. *Busy as a Bee*. Northborough, MA: Newbridge Educational Publishing, 1995.

_____. *Life in the Coral Reef*. New York, NY: Newbridge Educational Publishing, 1994.

Chandler Warner, Gertrude. *The Mystery of the Hidden Beach*. Morton Grove, IL: Albert Whitman & Company, 1994.

Rylant, Cynthia. *The Relatives Came*. New York, NY: Atheneum, 1985.

Poetry Resources

Children's Books

No More Homework, No More Tests by Bruce Lansky (Meadowbrook Press, 1997)

Falling Up by Shel Silverstein (HarperCollins, 1996)

Chicken Socks: And Other Contagious Poems by Brod Baggert (Boyds Mills Press, 2000)

The Gooch Machine: Poems for Children to Perform by Brod Baggert (Boyds Mills Press, 1997)

If You're Not Here, Please Raise Your Hand: Poems About School by Kalli Dakos (Aladdin, 1995)

It's Raining Pigs & Noodles by Jack Prelutsky (Greenwillow, 2000)

If Pigs Could Fly…and Other Deep Thoughts by Bruce Lansky (Meadowbrook Press, 2000)

Read-Aloud Rhymes for the Very Young edited by Jack Prelutsky (Alfred A. Knopf, 1986)

Professional Books

Poetry Place Anthology by Rosemary Alexander (Scholastic, 1999)

Index